Language Arts

Grade 3

Spark Educational Publishing
A Division of Barnes & Noble Publishing

Spark Educational Publishing
A Division of Barnes & Noble Publishing
120 Fifth Avenue
New York, NY 10011

Dear Parent,

This book was developed to help your child improve the language skills he or she needs to succeed. The book emphasizes skills in the key areas of:

- grammar
- punctuation
- vocabulary
- writing
- research

The more than 100 lessons included in the book provide many opportunities for your child to practice and apply important language and writing skills. These skills will help your child improve his or her communication abilities, excel in all academic areas, and increase his or her scores on standardized tests.

About the Book

The book is divided into six units:

- Parts of Speech
- Sentences
- Mechanics
- Vocabulary and Usage
- Writing
- Research Skills

Your child can work through each unit of the book, or you can pinpoint areas for extra practice.

Lessons have specific instructions and examples and are designed for your child to complete independently. Grammar lessons range from using nouns and verbs to constructing better sentences. Writing exercises range from the friendly letter to the research report. With this practice, your child will gain extra confidence as he or she works on daily school lessons or standardized tests.

A thorough answer key is also provided so you may check the quality of answers.

A Step toward Success

Practice may not always make perfect, but it is certainly a step in the right direction. The activities in this book are an excellent way to ensure greater success for your child.

Table of Contents

Nouns

A **noun** is a word that names a person, place, or thing.
Examples:

person = boy   **place** = store   **thing** = book

> **DIRECTIONS** ➤ **Complete each sentence with a noun from the box.**

| musician | forest | girl | stage | tree | flute |

1. The sound of a _____ floated through the theater.
(thing)

2. Another _____ began to play a horn.
(person)

3. Then, a boy appeared on the _____.
(place)

4. The boy hid behind a tall _____.
(thing)

5. A young _____ in a red dress walked onto the stage.
(person)

6. The boy pretended he was in a _____.
(place)

> **DIRECTIONS** ➤ **Think of a person, a place, and a thing. Write a sentence about each one on the line below.**

7. (person) _____

8. (place) _____

9. (thing) _____

Common Nouns and Proper Nouns

A **common noun** names any person, place, or thing. It begins with a lowercase letter.
Examples:

inventor   city   month

A **proper noun** names a particular person, place, or thing. Each important word of a proper noun begins with a capital letter.
Examples:

Thomas Alva Edison   Seattle   July

DIRECTIONS Read the paragraph below. Circle the common nouns. Underline the proper nouns.

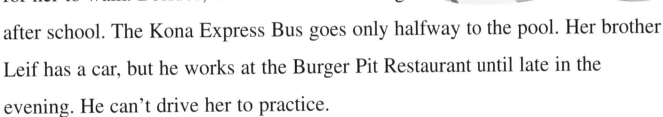

Maren wants to join the Kona Kai Swim Team, but she has a problem. She goes to Collins School on Miller Avenue. The school is three miles from the pool. That is too far for her to walk. Besides, she has to feed her dog after school. The Kona Express Bus goes only halfway to the pool. Her brother Leif has a car, but he works at the Burger Pit Restaurant until late in the evening. He can't drive her to practice.

DIRECTIONS Think of a common noun and a proper noun. Write a sentence about each one on the lines below.

(common noun) _____

(proper noun) _____

Common Nouns and Proper Nouns, page 2

Remember that a common noun names any person, place, or thing. It begins with a lowercase letter.
A proper noun names a particular person, place, or thing. Each important word of a proper noun begins with a capital letter.

 **DIRECTIONS** ⟶ **Read the sentences below. Circle the common nouns. Underline the proper nouns.**

1. Levi Hutchins was a clockmaker.

2. This young person lived in Concord, New Hampshire.

3. Hutchins always started to work early.

4. This fellow was awake before the sun came up.

5. Some people don't like to get up when the sky is dark.

6. The man had an idea for a new clock.

7. This machine would have a bell in it.

8. The owner would set the piece for a certain time.

9. A chime would ring then.

10. What invention did Hutchins create?

Common Nouns and Proper Nouns, page 3

 **DIRECTIONS** → **Read the paragraph below. Find all the common nouns and proper nouns. List them on the chart where they belong.**

Serena and Riane were very good musicians. They practiced at school and at home. One day they were invited to play at the Vallco Concert Hall. Mr. Williams was the leader of the Shadygrove Band. He thought that they had talent. He asked them to join his group.

PROPER NOUNS		
Person	Place	Thing

COMMON NOUNS		
Person	Place	Thing

Singular and Plural Nouns

A **singular noun** names one person, one place, or one thing.
Examples: friend   house   apple
A **plural noun** names more than one person, place, or thing.
Make most nouns plural by adding *s*.
Examples: friends   houses   apples

 **DIRECTIONS** Read the sentences below. Circle the singular nouns. Underline the plural nouns.

1. Badgers are skillful diggers.

2. A badger can dig a deep hole very quickly.

3. This mammal uses its front claws to dig.

4. A frightened animal might dig to get away from an enemy.

5. The mole also digs with powerful paws.

6. Its front legs work like shovels that scoop.

7. It digs long tunnels under bushes and trees.

8. This creature is very nearly blind.

9. This furry digger does not need to see well in its dark world.

10. Both badgers and moles are very good diggers.

Singular and Plural Nouns, page 2

Remember to use a **singular noun** to name one person, one place, or one thing. Use a **plural noun** to name more than one person, place, or thing. Add *s* to most singular nouns to form the plural.

DIRECTIONS → Write the plural form of the noun in ( ) to finish each sentence.

1. You can see many _____ on this farm.
   (animal)

2. The _____ take good care of them.
   (farmer)

3. The _____ are clucking loudly.
   (chicken)

4. There are _____ on the little lake.
   (duck)

5. You may see a few _____ there, too.
   (swan)

6. In the fields you will see _____.
   (cow)

7. The _____ are in the barn now.
   (horse)

8. Two _____ are following that sheep.
   (lamb)

9. Beyond the fence are some noisy _____.
   (goat)

10. Five big _____ are rolling in the mud.
    (pig)

11. The little _____ are just watching.
    (piglet)

Plural Nouns with *es*

Add *es* to form the plural of a noun ending with *s*, *x*, *ch*, or *sh*.
Examples:

bus	buses		box	boxes
branch	branches		brush	brushes

DIRECTIONS ▶ Write the plural form of each noun.

1. glass _____

2. dish _____

3. fox _____

4. patch _____

5. match _____

6. dress _____

7. lunch _____

8. tax _____

9. class _____

10. bush _____

DIRECTIONS ▶ Choose five of the plural nouns you wrote. Write your own sentences using those nouns on the lines.

11. _____

12. _____

13. _____

14. _____

15. _____

Plural Nouns with *ies*

If a noun ends in a consonant and *y*, change the *y* to *i* and add *es* to form the plural.
Examples:

   buddy   buddies   jelly   jellies

DIRECTIONS **Write the plural form of the noun in ( ) to finish each sentence.**

1. People who live in _____ enjoy parks.
(city)

2. Many _____ spend the day in the park.
(family)

3. Some people even have _____ there.
(party)

4. It is fun to see bright _____.
(butterfly)

5. It is even fun to see ants and _____ outdoors.
(fly)

6. Big dogs and little _____ run around.
(puppy)

7. The children hope to see _____.
(bunny)

8. Little _____ play in the grass.
(baby)

9. Older children pick _____ and other flowers.
(daisy)

10. Adults tell _____ and laugh.
(story)

Special Plural Nouns

Some nouns change spelling in the plural form.
Examples:

    man   men   foot feet   person people

DIRECTIONS ➤ **Read each sentence. Circle the noun in ( ) that fits best.**

1. Keisha has gone to Dr. Chun since she was a small (child, children).

2. The (man, men) who lives next door goes to Dr. Chun, too.

3. Dr. Chun is a fine dentist and a friendly (woman, women).

4. She has toys, including a wind-up (goose, geese), in her office.

5. Two of the toys are dancing (mouse, mice).

6. A big stuffed (ox, oxen) sits on a chair.

7. A cartoon about a little country (mouse, mice) hangs on the wall.

8. Two plastic (goose, geese) stand in the corner.

9. Many (child, children) like Dr. Chun.

10. She keeps her patients happy and their (tooth, teeth) healthy.

Singular Possessive Nouns

A **singular possessive noun** shows ownership by one person or thing.
Add an apostrophe (') and *s* to most singular nouns to show
possession.
Examples:

> Bob's dog   the dog's tail

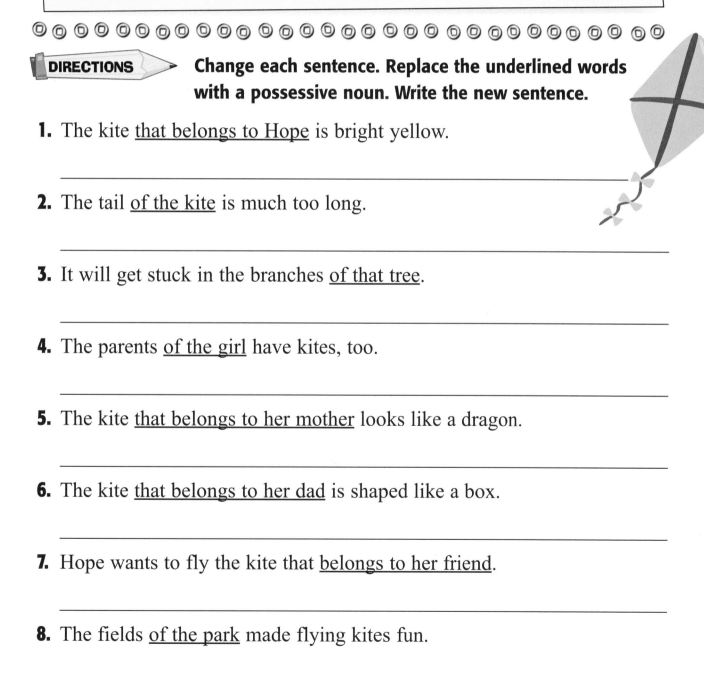

ⓄⓄⓄⓄⓄⓄⓄⓄⓄⓄⓄⓄⓄⓄⓄⓄⓄⓄⓄⓄⓄⓄⓄⓄⓄⓄⓄ

DIRECTIONS ▷ Change each sentence. Replace the underlined words
with a possessive noun. Write the new sentence.

1. The kite <u>that belongs to Hope</u> is bright yellow.

_____

2. The tail <u>of the kite</u> is much too long.

_____

3. It will get stuck in the branches <u>of that tree</u>.

_____

4. The parents <u>of the girl</u> have kites, too.

_____

5. The kite <u>that belongs to her mother</u> looks like a dragon.

_____

6. The kite <u>that belongs to her dad</u> is shaped like a box.

_____

7. Hope wants to fly the kite that <u>belongs to her friend</u>.

_____

8. The fields <u>of the park</u> made flying kites fun.

_____

Plural Possessive Nouns

A **plural possessive noun** shows ownership by more than one person or thing. To form most plural possessive nouns, add an apostrophe (') to the end of a plural noun.
Examples:

  cars' engines   grandparents' ranch   children's lunches

 **DIRECTIONS** Read the paragraph below. Circle the plural nouns that show ownership.

The chickens' clucking woke Jason. In the distance, he heard a fox's high bark. Jason and his grandfather checked all the animals' pens. By the chicken coop, they saw several foxes' paw prints. Luckily, none of the chickens had been harmed.

DIRECTIONS Write the possessive form of each plural noun shown in ( ) below.

1. Oscar followed the _____ footprints to the pond.
        (squirrels)

2. He found his four _____ shoes by the pond.
        (brothers)

3. The _____ loud barks made him look up into the trees.
        (dogs)

4. His brothers were sitting high up on the _____ limbs.
        (trees)

Singular and Plural Possessive Nouns

Remember that a possessive noun shows ownership.
Add an apostrophe (') and *s* to most singular nouns to show possession.
To form most plural possessive nouns, add an apostrophe (') to the end of a plural noun.

DIRECTIONS Underline the possessive noun in each sentence. On the line, write whether it is singular or plural.

1. The table's leg was loose. _____

2. The dog's wagging tail thumped against the table. _____

3. The families' homemade cookies fell to the ground. _____

4. The picnickers' dessert was ruined! _____

5. The ripe blackberries' smell was sweet. _____

6. Danny borrowed Adam's bowl. _____

7. The children filled their grandparents'

buckets with berries. _____

8. The bike's tire was flat. _____

Pronouns

A **pronoun** is a word that takes the place of one or more nouns.
Examples:

    Little Elk had a gift for painting.
    He had a gift for painting.
    He takes the place of *Little Elk*.

    The warriors admired Little Elk.
    They admired Little Elk.
    They takes the place of *the warriors*.

DIRECTIONS   Read each pair of sentences. Circle the pronoun in the second sentence. Write which word or words from the first sentence it replaces.

1. Little Elk loved to look at clouds.
He felt joy from studying the sky.

_____

2. Sometimes Little Elk's mother worried. She knew Little Elk was different.

_____

3. One day Little Elk found some soil. He mixed the soil with rain water.

_____

4. Little Elk later made a blue paint. It was the color of the sky.

_____

Singular Pronouns

A **singular pronoun** replaces a singular noun. The words *I, me, you, he, she, him, her,* and *it* are singular pronouns. Always capitalize the pronoun *I*.

Examples:

Jorge, have *you* ever seen picture writing?
You stands for *Jorge*.

I learned about picture writing from my grandfather.
I replaces the speaker's name.

He studied *it* in Arizona.
He stands for *my grandfather*. *It* replaces *picture writing*.

DIRECTIONS ⟩ **Read each pair of sentences. Write the singular pronoun that fits with the meaning of the second sentence.**

1. Ned was going to a soccer match. _____ wore a jacket.

2. Ned's mom had been reading. She had brought a newspaper with _____ .

3. Ned got on the train. Ned's mom followed _____ .

4. Ned's mom studied a map. _____ told Ned they would get off at the next stop.

5. A moment later, the train slowed down. _____ was at the station.

6. Ned held tight as the train stopped. Soon, _____ got off the train.

Plural Pronouns

A **plural pronoun** replaces a plural noun. The words *we, you, they, us,* and *them* are plural pronouns.
Examples:

    People use colors in many ways.
    They use colors in many ways.
    They replaces *people.*

    Artists use colors in paintings.
    Artists use *them* in paintings.
    Them replaces *colors.*

DIRECTIONS ▷ **Revise each sentence. Replace each word or group of words in ( ) with a plural pronoun.**

1. (My dad and I) _____ like the

work of early American artists.

2. My dad knows a lot about (many early American

artists) _____.

3. (Early American painters) _____

sometimes painted on wooden boards.

4. The artists made (paints) _____ from plants and rocks.

5. (A master and a student) _____ often worked together.

6. Going to museums is fun for (my dad and me) _____.

Singular and Plural Pronouns

Remember, a singular pronoun replaces a singular noun. The words *I, me, you, he, she, him, her,* and *it* are singular pronouns. Always capitalize the pronoun *I.*

A plural pronoun replaces a plural noun. The words *we, you, they, us,* and *them* are plural pronouns.

DIRECTIONS Read each pair of sentences. Write the pronoun that fits best in the second sentence of each pair. Use the clue in ( ) to help you.

1. Piñatas are popular in Mexico.

_____ are hollow toys made from paper.
     (plural)

2. Piñatas come in many shapes.

Often _____ are shaped like animals.
          (plural)

3. The piñata hangs from the ceiling.

_____ contains gifts and treats.
     (singular)

4. Anita tries to hit the piñata with a stick.

_____ has been blindfolded.
     (singular)

5. The children cheer when the piñata breaks.

_____ rush to collect the prizes.
     (plural)

Subject Pronouns

A **subject pronoun** takes the place of one or more nouns in the subject of a sentence. The words *I*, *you*, *he*, *she*, *it*, *we*, and *they* are subject pronouns.
Examples:

> *They* brought a snake to school.
> *I* do not like snakes.
> *You* can hold the snake.

 **DIRECTIONS** Read the paragraph below. Look at the words in dark letters. Circle the ones that are singular subject pronouns. Underline the one that is a plural subject pronoun.

My name is Meredyth. **I** love to paint. My mother helped me set up an easel. **She** hangs my pictures around the house. "**They** brighten up the walls," Mom says. My father thinks that **I** am a good artist, too. "**You** will be famous someday," Dad says. **He** is my biggest fan.

 **DIRECTIONS** Write each pronoun you circled or underlined in the chart below. Next to it, write the word or words the pronoun replaces.

Subject Pronoun	Word or Words It Replaces

Object Pronouns

An **object pronoun** follows an action verb, such as *see* or *tell*, or a word such as *about, at, for, from, near, of, to,* or *with*.
The words *me, you, him, her, it, us,* and *them* are object pronouns.
Examples:

Sam took *it* home.
Mom had a surprise for *me*.
My friend saw *you*.

 **DIRECTIONS** Complete this story. Write an object pronoun that replaces the underlined word or words.

Mom left <u>my brother and me</u> at home. She trusted

_____. Our mother went to see <u>her parents</u>. She had some

presents for _____. <u>Mom</u> waved from the car window. We

stood on the porch and waved back to _____. <u>My older

brother</u> was in charge. I had to listen to _____.

After a while, we heard a knock on <u>the door</u>. I asked my brother to

open _____.

"I hope that's not <u>your silly friends</u>," my brother said. "I don't want to

see _____ on our porch."

I knew <u>my brother</u> wouldn't really be mad. So I asked

_____ again to open the door. <u>My friends</u> were there.

_____ were wearing big wolf masks. For just a minute,

my brother was afraid of _____.

I and Me

Use the word *I* as a subject pronoun.
Use the word *me* as an object pronoun.
Examples:

   I could not find my lunch.
   My brother helped *me*.

DIRECTIONS ➤ **Finish each sentence. Write the correct word or words in ( ).**

1. _____ play baseball every day.
(My friends and me, My friends and I)

2. Sometimes students from other schools play with _____.
(we, us)

3. _____ take turns pitching.
(Nell and me, Nell and I)

4. Usually, _____ are the first
(Casey and me, Casey and I)
batters up.

5. My parents like to practice with _____.
(I, me)

6. Mom pitches the ball to _____.
(I, me)

7. Then _____ hit it as hard as I can.
(I, me)

8. Dad always runs after the ball for _____.
(I, me)

9. He tosses the ball back to _____.
(Mom and me, Mom and I)

10. _____ have fun playing baseball.
(My parents and me, My parents and I)

Possessive Pronouns

A **possessive pronoun** shows ownership. Some possessive pronouns are *my*, *your*, *his*, *her*, *its*, *our*, and *their*.

Examples:

Chipper is *my* horse.
He lives in *our* barn.
Where is *your* pet?

DIRECTIONS ▷ **Read each sentence. Circle the possessive pronoun.**

1. Tonya shouted to her friends.

2. "Please come to our apartment this afternoon," she said.

3. Tonya explained, "My family is having a party."

4. Victor asked, "Will your grandfather be there?"

5. "Yes," said Tonya, "and he's bringing two of his brothers."

6. "Mom and Dad are having the party for their anniversary," she said.

7. She went on, "I get to wear my new red shoes."

8. "Even the dog will be wearing its shiny new collar," Tonya said.

DIRECTIONS ▷ **Finish each sentence. Write a possessive pronoun that makes sense.**

9. Victor said to Tonya, "I like seeing _____ grandfather."

10. Victor explained, "_____ grandparents live far away, and I hardly ever see them."

11. Tonya smiled and nodded _____ head.

Contractions with Pronouns

A **contraction** is a short way of writing two words together. Some of the letters are left out. An apostrophe (') takes the place of the missing letters.

Form some contractions by joining pronouns and verbs.

Examples:

I + am = *I'm*   you + are = *you're*   she + is = *she's*

 **DIRECTIONS** ➤ **Write each sentence. Replace the underlined words with a contraction.**

1. <u>It is</u> dark and cold outside.

_____

2. <u>You are</u> in a hurry.

_____

3. You hear noises, but <u>they are</u> far away.

_____

4. Now <u>they have</u> become louder.

_____

5. Something is behind you, and <u>it is</u> getting closer.

_____

6. "<u>I will</u> just go a little faster," you think.

_____

7. Now <u>you are</u> almost running.

_____

8. <u>You will</u> be home in just a few minutes.

_____

Adjectives

An **adjective** is a word that describes a noun. Adjectives can tell how many, what color, or what size or shape. They can also describe how something feels, sounds, tastes, or smells.
Use exact adjectives to paint clear word pictures.
Examples:

Three birds were in the nest.
The *red* ball was in a *small* box.
The *smooth* soap has a *sweet* smell.

DIRECTIONS ➤ **Write the adjective that describes each underlined noun.**

1. The Vikings lived in small <u>villages</u>. _____

2. Many <u>houses</u> were built around a main house. _____

3. The main <u>building</u> was like a barn. _____

4. The roof was held up by heavy <u>beams</u>. _____

5. The walls were made of split <u>trunks</u> of trees. _____

6. These trunks were set in a double <u>layer</u>. _____

7. One end of the central <u>house</u> was for people. _____

8. The other <u>half</u> of the building was for cattle. _____

9. A wooden <u>screen</u> divided the house. _____

10. In the middle of the hall was a big <u>fire</u>. _____

Adjectives That Tell How Many

Remember that some adjectives tell how many.
Some adjectives that tell how many do not tell an exact number.
Examples:

A horse runs on *four* legs.
That horse has been in *many* shows.

◎◎◎◎◎◎◎◎◎◎◎◎◎◎◎◎◎◎◎◎◎◎◎◎◎◎◎◎◎◎◎◎◎◎◎◎

DIRECTIONS ➤ **Read each sentence. Write the adjective that tells how many.**

1. Two monkeys were in the room. _____

2. Several boxes were also in the room. _____

3. Some bananas were hanging from the ceiling. _____

4. After a few hours, the monkeys piled up the boxes. _____

5. They were able to reach the eight bananas. _____

DIRECTIONS ➤ **Write an exact number word to complete each sentence. Then, write the sentence again, using an adjective that does not tell an exact number.**

6. Anna wanted _____ pets.

_____

7. She asked for _____ monkeys.

_____

8. We saw _____ monkeys at the zoo.

_____

◎◎◎◎◎◎◎◎◎◎◎◎◎◎◎◎◎◎◎◎◎◎◎◎◎◎◎◎◎◎◎

Adjectives That Tell What Kind

Remember that some adjectives tell what kind.
They can describe size, shape, or color. They can help you know how something looks, sounds, feels, tastes, or smells.
Examples:

A *tall* woman stands on the corner.
She wears a *red* hat.
This *quiet* detective is Madame Girard.
Tiny cameras are hidden in her hat.

DIRECTIONS → **In each sentence, circle the adjective that tells what kind. Write the noun it describes.**

1. Madame Girard also uses tiny computers. _____

2. She keeps them in her secret pouch. _____

3. She takes careful notes on her cases. _____

4. Notes help her solve difficult mysteries. _____

5. She once found lost diamonds. _____

6. Yesterday she found Lulu's famous parrot. _____

7. Today Madame Girard lost an important key. _____

8. Lulu helped her embarrassed friend find it. _____

DIRECTIONS → **Write a sentence using each adjective below.**

9. (green) _____

10. (huge) _____

Predicate Adjectives

An adjective is a word that describes a noun. A **predicate adjective** follows a verb such as *is*, *seems*, or *looks*.

Examples:

That whale is *huge*.

That lion looks *scary*.

DIRECTIONS Circle the adjective in each sentence. Tell which noun it describes.

1. Yosemite Park is beautiful. _____

2. The views there are incredible! _____

3. This mountain is difficult to climb. _____

4. This tree seems taller than the other one. _____

5. The sky was blue. _____

6. From an airplane, houses look tiny. _____

7. The man feels sick. _____

8. That dog was mean. _____

9. The flower smelled sweet. _____

10. The cat feels soft. _____

Articles

The words *a*, *an*, and *the* are called **articles**.
Use *a* before a word that begins with a consonant sound.
Use *an* before a word that begins with a vowel sound.
Use *the* before a word that begins with a consonant or a vowel.
Examples:

> Have you ever seen *an* owl?
> *The* owl is *a* nocturnal animal.

DIRECTIONS ➤ **Read the following paragraph. Circle the articles.**

Last week my mother and I saw an owl in the trees behind our house. It was evening, and the air was just beginning to turn cool. We were walking down a gravel path from the shed to our house. Suddenly, we heard a strange sound. My mother froze, her eyes on an old pine tree. I followed her eyes and caught a glimpse of the owl as it took off.

DIRECTIONS ➤ **Complete each sentence by circling the correct article in ( ).**

1. My teacher assigned (a / an) report about wild animals.

2. I'm going to write about (a / an) bald eagle.

3. I once saw (a / an) eagle when I was camping with my family.

4. My mother says that bald eagles are (a / an) endangered species.

5. (A / An) cat next door likes to watch birds.

Adjectives That Compare: *er, est*

Add *er* to most short adjectives to compare two nouns or pronouns.

Add *est* to most short adjectives to compare more than two nouns or pronouns.

Change the *y* to *i* before adding *er* or *est* to adjectives that end in a consonant and *y*.

Examples:

This tree is *greener* than that one.

The whale is the *largest* of all animals.

She was the *happiest* student in class.

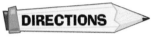

DIRECTIONS → **Choose the correct form of the adjective in ( ) to complete each sentence. Write the adjective on the line.**

1. Town Mouse was _____ than his cousin.
(richer, richest)

2. One day he visited Country Mouse in the _____
(poorer, poorest)

village of the land.

3. Town Mouse was _____ than his cousin,
(younger, youngest)

but he was used to much better cooking.

4. Town Mouse said, "I want you to visit my house. It's
_____ than yours."
(fancier, fanciest)

5. Town Mouse said, "I'm _____ than a bear after a
(hungrier, hungriest)

long winter!"

6. The two mice went into the _____ dining room
(grander, grandest)

Country Mouse had ever seen.

Adjectives That Compare: *more, most*

Use *more* with some adjectives to compare two nouns or pronouns.
Use *most* with some adjectives to compare more than two nouns or pronouns.

Examples:

Parrots are *more talkative* than parakeets.

I am the *most athletic* of everyone in my family.

DIRECTIONS ⟶ **Write *more* or *most* to complete each sentence.**

1. Diving may be the _____ difficult of all sports.

2. It is _____ interesting to watch than golf.

3. A diver hits the water in the _____ graceful way possible.

4. A high dive is _____ dangerous than a low one.

5. I saw the _____ amazing dive at a meet.

6. That was the _____ skillful dive I have ever seen.

7. This year's swimming meet was _____ exciting than last year's.

8. The winner was perhaps the _____ powerful swimmer I have ever seen.

9. I am _____ skilled at diving than my sister.

10. He is the _____ talented diver I know.

More about Adjectives That Compare

Adjectives can describe by comparing people, animals, places, or things. Add *er* to adjectives to compare two things, or use the word *more*. Add *est* to adjectives to compare more than two things, or use the word *most*.

DIRECTIONS **Read the following paragraph. Underline the adjectives that make comparisons.**

I think a walk outside is more interesting than an hour of TV. I enjoy trying to spot different birds in the forest. Some birds are rarer than others. For example, owls are the most difficult birds to find. Blue jays are bolder than many birds, so they are easier to spot.

DIRECTIONS **Circle the correct form of the adjective in ( ).**

1. I think dogs are (friendlier / friendliest) than cats.

2. My dog looks (happier / happiest) than my cat when I get home.

3. Dogs are (most / more) obedient than cats.

4. On the other hand, cats are (easier / easiest) to hold in your lap than dogs are.

5. I don't like birds because they are the (noisiest / noisier) kind of pet to have.

Verbs

A **verb** is a word that shows action.

A verb is the main word in the predicate of a sentence. A verb and its subject should agree.

Examples:

Frogs *live* the first part of their lives as water animals.

They *spend* the rest of their lives as land animals.

 **DIRECTIONS** Circle the verb in each sentence.

1. Tadpoles begin their lives underwater.

2. A tadpole's body changes over time.

3. Its tail grows long.

4. The back legs kick.

5. Next, the front legs develop.

6. Tadpoles breathe through gills.

7. An older tadpole loses its gills and its tail.

8. The change becomes complete.

9. A tiny frog climbs onto land.

10. The new frog appears as a land animal.

Action Verbs

An **action verb** is a word that shows action.

An action verb is the main word in the predicate of a sentence. An action verb is a word that tells what the subject of a sentence does.

Examples:

Many fruits *grow* in the United States.

My dad *eats* bananas for lunch.

DIRECTIONS → **Read each sentence. Write the action verb.**

1. I peek through the curtains at the yard.

_____

2. The snow covers the ground with a thick

white blanket. _____

3. Eagerly I go outside. _____

4. I close the door quickly behind me.

_____

5. I walk in the freezing air. _____

6. My feet crunch in the new snow. _____

7. The cold wind nips my nose. _____

8. I build a huge snow castle. _____

9. Then, I return to my warm house. _____

10. I remove my coat and mittens. _____

Main Verbs

Sometimes the predicate has two or more verbs. The **main verb** is the most important verb in a sentence.

Examples:

One type of bird <u>has *become*</u> an excellent swimmer.

Those penguins <u>have *dived*</u> many times to the ocean floor.

DIRECTIONS ▷ **Circle the main verb in each sentence.**

1. That squirrel has floated through the air!

2. It has landed safely in a tree.

3. Juan has disappeared inside the house.

4. He had passed his video camera to me.

5. We have taped some amazing animals.

6. This flying squirrel had played a starring role.

7. Have you noticed this picture?

8. The squirrel's body has changed into a glider.

9. It had soared from tree to tree.

10. We have waited for the squirrel's next flight.

Helping Verbs

A **helping verb** can work with the main verb to tell about an action. The helping verb always comes before the main verb. The words *have*, *has*, and *had* are often used as helping verbs.
Examples:
My dad *had* studied all kinds of flight.
We *have* gone on a balloon flight together.

DIRECTIONS → **In each sentence, circle the helping verb. Then, write the verb it is helping.**

1. My dad has owned many types of flying machines.

_____

2. We have traveled in most of them together. _____

3. We had soared over the land in hot-air balloons and gliders.

_____

4. We have wanted a very special plane. _____

5. I had looked at pictures of this plane in history books.

_____

6. Our plane has finally landed at the town airport! _____

7. We have replaced many of its parts. _____

8. Dad had painted it. _____

9. People have called us from all over the country. _____

10. Dad has planned a party in honor of the special old plane.

_____

Main and Helping Verbs

Remember that the main verb is the most important verb in a sentence. The helping verb works with the main verb to tell about an action.

DIRECTIONS ▷ **Circle the main verb and underline the helping verb in each sentence.**

Troy has traveled to Mexico. I have visited that country, too. Troy and I have read many books about Mexican history together. I had planned a trip there with Troy. But my teacher has given me too much work, and I have stayed home. Troy has written me a postcard.

DIRECTIONS ▷ **Circle the correct helping verb in ( ).**

1. Teo (has / have) lived in Amarillo for ten years.

2. He (have / has) built a house at the edge of the city.

3. Teo's parents also (has / have) built a nice home there.

4. I (have / has) sent a letter to Teo.

DIRECTIONS ▷ **Write a sentence about a place you have visited. Use a helping verb in your sentence.**

_____

_____

_____

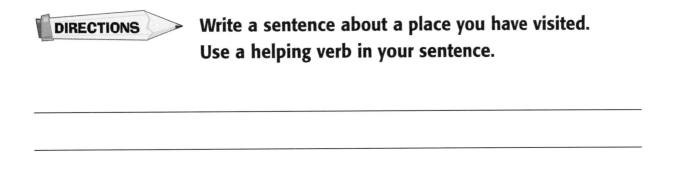

Present-Tense Verbs

A **present-tense verb** tells about actions that are happening now.
Add *s* or *es* to most present-tense verbs when the subject of the
sentence is *he*, *she*, *it*, or a singular noun.
Do not add *s* or *es* to a present-tense verb when
the subject is *I*, *you*, *we*, *they*, or a plural noun.
Examples:

She *flies* a jet.
Many women *fly* planes today.

 **DIRECTIONS** ▷ Complete each sentence with a present-tense verb from the box.

take	takes	drive	drives	chase	chases
play	plays	drink	drinks	watch	watches

1. My grandparents _____ to our vacation cabin.

2. My aunt _____ her car there, too.

3. I _____ icy lemonade.

4. Mom _____ iced tea.

5. Eddie and I _____ catch.

6. Then we _____ each other around the yard.

7. Our dog Mondo _____ us silently.

8. He _____ the ball from us.

9. Alicia _____ a game of checkers with Mom.

10. We _____ the sun go down.

Past-Tense Verbs

A **past-tense verb** tells about actions that happened in the past.
Add *ed* or *d* to most present-tense verbs to make them show past tense.
Examples:

Last winter it *snowed* heavily.
The snow *covered* the ground.
We *played* in the snow.

 **DIRECTIONS** ⟩ **Write the past-tense verb from each sentence on the line.
Circle the ending that makes the verb show past tense.**

1. It rained last night. _____

2. We closed all the windows quickly. _____

3. Thunder crashed outside. _____

4. The dog barked at the loud noise. _____

5. I watched the lightning. _____

6. Rain poured from the roof. _____

7. The roof leaked in two places. _____

8. We placed buckets under the leaks. _____

9. My mother started a fire in the fireplace. _____

10. We listened to the storm. _____

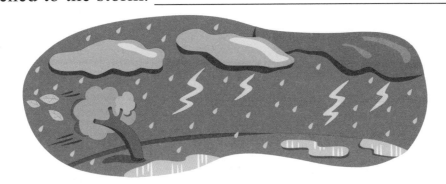

Present-Tense and Past-Tense Verbs

Remember that a present-tense verb tells about actions that are happening now.

A past-tense verb tells about actions that happened in the past.

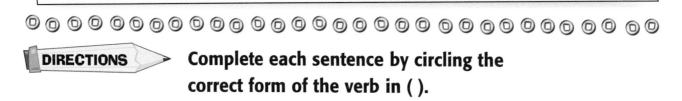

DIRECTIONS ➤ Complete each sentence by circling the correct form of the verb in ( ).

1. Seals (eat / eats) squid and fish.

2. Most seals (lives / live) along the coast.

3. The northern fur seal (spend / spends) the summer

near Alaska.

4. Soft fur (covers / cover) the body of a seal pup.

5. A seal (swim / swims) by using both its front and rear flippers.

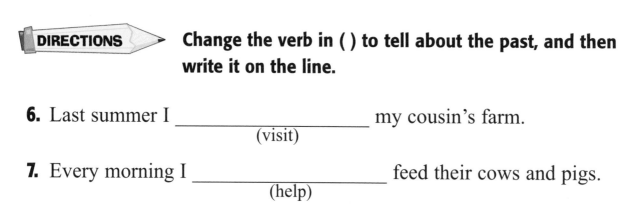

DIRECTIONS ➤ Change the verb in ( ) to tell about the past, and then write it on the line.

6. Last summer I _____ my cousin's farm.
     (visit)

7. Every morning I _____ feed their cows and pigs.
     (help)

8. I _____ working with animals.
     (enjoy)

9. My aunt _____ a big breakfast.
     (cook)

10. I _____ the smell of bacon and eggs.
     (like)

Irregular Verbs

An **irregular verb** is a verb that does not end with *ed* to show past tense.

Examples:

Present	Past	Past with Helping Verb
do, does	did	(have, has, had) done
drive, drives	drove	(have, has, had) driven
eat, eats	ate	(have, has, had) eaten
go, goes	went	(have, has, had) gone

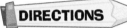 **DIRECTIONS**   Circle the correct verb in ( ) to complete each sentence.

1. We had (drives / driven) for hours.

2. We (came / comes) to a picnic area in a little valley.

3. We (ate / eats) lunch at the base of Mount St. Helens.

4. Mom (go / went) to get her guidebook.

5. People (drove / driven) away fast when the volcano erupted in 1980.

6. After the eruption, many (come / came) back to rebuild.

7. The eruption of Mount St. Helens (do / did) things to help the ecosystem.

8. I want to (went / go) back one day.

More Irregular Verbs

Remember that an irregular verb is a verb that does not end with *ed* to show past tense. Use special forms of the verbs *eat*, *give*, *grow*, *know*, *take*, and *write* to show past tense.

DIRECTIONS → Finish each sentence. Write the correct form of the irregular verb in ( ).

1. Aunt Celia _____ me a camera.
(gave, given)

2. I _____ her a thank-you note.
(wrote, written)

3. She _____ just what I wanted.
(knew, known)

4. I have _____ many pictures.
(took, taken)

5. My brother _____ three inches.
(grew, grown)

6. I _____ many pictures of him.
(took, taken)

7. Our family _____ dinner.
(ate, eaten)

8. I _____ pictures of everyone.
(took, taken)

9. After we had _____, I showed some of my best pictures.
(ate, eaten)

10. I had _____ a story to go with the pictures.
(wrote, written)

Linking Verbs

A **linking verb** connects the subject with words in the predicate of a sentence. It tells what the subject is or is like.
Forms of the verb *be* are often used as linking verbs.
Use *am*, *is*, and *are* to show present tense.
Use *was* and *were* to show past tense.
Examples:

That girl *is* a kind person.
The man *was* lonely.

DIRECTIONS Read each sentence. Circle the verb. Then write *be* if the verb is a form of *be*. Write *action* if the verb is an action verb.

1. Many kinds of animals live in trees. _____

2. That huge nest is a home for chimpanzees. _____

3. Those bird nests are empty now. _____

4. Sometimes squirrels use old bird nests. _____

5. Hollow trees are also good homes for squirrels. _____

6. The hummingbirds were away all winter. _____

7. One hummingbird is back now._____

8. I am very happy about that. _____

9. Hummingbirds are tiny. _____

10. They build very small nests. _____

Adverbs

An **adverb** is a word that describes a verb.
An adverb may tell *when* or *where* an action happens.
Examples:

      Today we visited a theme park.
      We ran *ahead*, and our parents followed.

DIRECTIONS — **Circle the adverb in each sentence. Then, write if the adverb tells *when* or *where*.**

1. We see Thomas Edison's inventions everywhere.

    _____

2. His achievements can be found here. _____

3. You often use his inventions. _____

4. Without him, you could never turn on a light. _____

5. Films are always shown through one of his inventions. _____

DIRECTIONS — **Complete each sentence by adding an adverb. Choose from the adverbs in ( ).**

6. Edison _____ worked for many days without stopping.
             (often, there)

7. He _____ improved the inventions of others.
      (around, sometimes)

8. _____ he became known as the world's greatest inventor.
    (Soon, Here)

More Adverbs

Remember that an adverb is a word that describes a verb.
Some adverbs tell *how* about a verb. Many adverbs that tell how end in *ly*.
Examples:

   My sister screamed *loudly*.
   We ran *quickly* to the cave.

DIRECTIONS → **Write the adverb in each sentence.**

1. Edith and Carol ran swiftly to the train. _____

2. They climbed on board quickly. _____

3. Breathlessly, they took the nearest seats. _____

4. Luckily, they had arrived on time. _____

5. They had excitedly planned this little trip. _____

6. They had foolishly waited until the last minute to go to the station.

_____

7. The train ran exactly on time. _____

8. Fortunately, there had been little traffic.

_____

9. Carol and Edith had barely made it.

_____

10. They looked happily out the window.

_____

Using Adverbs

DIRECTIONS ▷ **Choose the adverb from the box that best fits in each blank below. Use the clues in ( ) to help you.**

often	carefully	cleverly	downstairs

My grandmother is a woodcarver. She keeps her tools

_____ in the basement. She _____
(Where?)   (When?)

works on her carving after we eat dinner. With a carving tool in hand, she

_____ cuts the wood. After a week or two, she has
(How?)

_____ carved something beautiful.
(How?)

DIRECTIONS ▷ **Finish each sentence by writing an adverb that tells *where*, *when*, or *how*. Use your own words.**

1. Our family listens to the radio _____.
(When?)

2. Sometimes we listen to the radio _____.
(Where?)

3. We heard a new commercial for milk _____.
(When?)

4. Five cows were singing _____.
(How?)

5. Dad started laughing _____.
(How?)

Good and Well

Students often have trouble with *good* and *well*.
Use *good* as an adjective.
Use *well* most often as an adverb.
Examples:
> I did a *good* job on my report.
> I write *well*.

DIRECTIONS ▷ **Read each sentence. If the underlined word is used correctly, write *correct*. If not, write the sentence correctly.**

1. Doris went with her mother to see a <u>good</u> movie.

_____

2. They sat in the middle so they could see and hear <u>good</u>.

_____

3. The actors in the movie played their parts <u>good</u>.

_____

4. Doris and her mother shared some very <u>well</u> popcorn.

_____

5. The movie was based on a <u>good</u> book Doris had read.

_____

DIRECTIONS ▷ **Write *good* or *well* to complete each sentence.**

6. Doris and her mother had a _____ time that day.

7. Doris and her mother always got along _____.

8. They had especially _____ times on Saturdays.

What Is a Sentence?

A **sentence** is a group of words that tells a complete thought.
The words in the sentence should be in an order that makes sense.
Begin every sentence with a capital letter, and end it with the correct end mark.
Examples:

Most plants grow from seeds.
A strawberry's seeds are on its skin.

 **DIRECTIONS** Read each group of words. If the group is a sentence, draw a line under it.

1. Dinosaurs lived long ago.
2. The biggest dinosaur of all.
3. Some dinosaurs were small.
4. No bigger than a chicken.
5. Not all dinosaurs ate meat.
6. Leaves and other parts of plants.
7. Tyrannosaurus Rex had big teeth.
8. Dinosaur bones in museums.

 **DIRECTIONS** Choose two groups of words you did not underline. Add words to make each group a sentence. Write the sentences you make.

9. _____

_____

10. _____

_____

Parts of a Sentence

A sentence has several parts.
The **subject** names something or someone in the sentence.
The **predicate** tells what the subject is or does.
Examples:
  Birds eat fruit from trees and vines. (subject)
  They *drop the seeds onto the ground*. (predicate)

 **DIRECTIONS** ➤ **Read each sentence. Write *subject* if the subject is underlined. Write *predicate* if the predicate is underlined.**

1. <u>Our class</u> made flowers out of paper. _____

2. <u>Mr. Sanchez</u> brought us many kinds of paper. _____

3. Brad <u>folded a yellow handkerchief</u>. _____

4. <u>He</u> tied it with a green wire. _____

5. His flower <u>was a carnation</u>. _____

6. Three girls <u>cut circles out of tissue paper</u>. _____

7. <u>Nina</u> glued the circles together. _____

8. Her friends <u>curled the edges</u>. _____

9. <u>The girls</u> added green paper stems. _____

10. Everyone <u>likes our paper garden</u>. _____

Subjects

Every sentence has a **subject**. The subject is the part of the sentence about which something is said.
The subject is usually at the beginning of a sentence.
Examples:

Seeds travel in different ways.
Some of these seeds grow into plants.

DIRECTIONS **Write the subject of each sentence.**

1. Some seeds are carried by the wind.

_____

2. Dandelion seeds are light and puffy.

_____

3. The wind carries them a long way.

_____

4. They float through the air.

_____

5. Pioneers carried seeds with them.

_____

6. These settlers planted the seeds.

_____

7. Some families planned orchards.

_____

8. The wilderness disappeared slowly.

_____

Predicates

Every sentence has a **predicate**. The predicate is the part of the sentence that tells what the subject of the sentence is or does. The predicate is usually the last part of the sentence.
Examples:

Samantha Sanders *is the bravest kid in my class.*
She *thinks of a new adventure every week.*

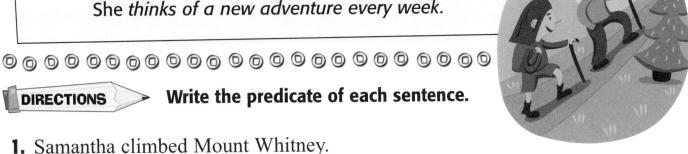

DIRECTIONS ▷ **Write the predicate of each sentence.**

1. Samantha climbed Mount Whitney.

_____

2. Mount Whitney is in California.

_____

3. Samantha went there with her father.

_____

4. They climbed for one whole day.

_____

5. Samantha took pictures of snow at the top.

_____

6. Samantha went rafting on the Snake River.

_____

7. The river bucked like a wild horse.

_____

8. She loved the exciting ride.

_____

Subjects and Predicates

Remember that every sentence has a subject that names the person or thing the sentence is about.

Every sentence has a predicate that tells what the subject of the sentence is or does.

 **DIRECTIONS** → **Underline the subject in each sentence. Circle the predicate in each sentence.**

1. New York City is the largest city in the United States.

2. More than 7 million people live in New York City.

3. New Yorkers come from many different backgrounds.

4. The subway system runs on about 230 miles of track.

5. The city is a center for trade, business, and the arts.

6. Millions of people visit New York City every year.

7. Theater is one of the city's most popular art forms.

8. Many visitors attend Broadway shows.

9. One tall building in New York City is the Empire State Building.

10. The Statue of Liberty stands on an island in New York Harbor.

11. This monument is a symbol of freedom.

12. Tourists take pictures of the statue.

Statements and Questions

A **statement** is a sentence that tells something.
Use a period (.) at the end of a statement.
A **question** is a sentence that asks something.
Use a question mark (?) at the end of a question.
Begin every statement or question with a capital letter.
Examples:
  Luther Burbank was a famous gardener.
  Where did Luther Burbank live?

 **DIRECTIONS** ➤ Write each statement or question so that it begins and ends correctly. Then circle *S* if the sentence is a statement or *Q* if it is a question.

1. do you like gardens   S   Q

_____

2. we planted vegetables here   S   Q

_____

3. do the plants need water   S   Q

_____

4. who will pull the weeds   S   Q

_____

5. these tomatoes look good   S   Q

_____

6. are they ripe   S   Q

_____

7. this tomato is bright red   S   Q

_____

Exclamations and Commands

An **exclamation** is a sentence that shows strong feeling.
Use an exclamation point (!) at the end of an exclamation.
A **command** is a sentence that gives an order or a direction.
Use a period (.) at the end of a command.
Examples:

 Wow, what a huge blackberry!
 Don't pick those berries.

DIRECTIONS Write each exclamation or command so that it begins and ends correctly. Then circle *E* if the sentence is an exclamation or *C* if it is a command.

1. watch my pet fish   E   C

_____

2. he's amazing   E   C

_____

3. see how he follows my directions   E   C

_____

4. swim through the hoop, Finny   E   C

_____

5. now dive to the bottom   E   C

_____

6. you're terrific, Finny   E   C

_____

7. swim around in big circles   E   C

_____

Capital Letters and End Marks in Sentences

Begin each sentence with a capital letter.
End statements and commands with a period (.).
End a question with a question mark (?).
End an exclamation with an exclamation point (!).

DIRECTIONS ▶ **Add the correct end mark to each sentence.**

1. Do you wonder who made the first comb _____

2. The earliest combs were found in Egyptian tombs 6,000 years old _____

3. Look at that unusual comb _____

4. If you found a 6,000-year-old comb, would you use it _____

5. What an old comb that would be _____

DIRECTIONS ▶ **Use capital letters and end marks to separate the sentences in each pair. Write the sentences on the lines.**

6. Most early people used combs the only ones who didn't were the Britons

_____

_____

7. Does it make you wonder how they looked the Britons left their hair messy

_____

_____

8. I comb my hair every day do you

_____

_____

Agreement of Subjects with the Verb *Be*

The predicate of a sentence must agree with the subject in number.
Use *am*, *is*, and *was* with singular subjects.
Use *are* and *were* with plural subjects.
Examples:

The *dog is* gone.
My *friends were* afraid of it.

DIRECTIONS → **Write *am*, *is*, or *are* to finish each sentence.**

1. I _____ a pet.

2. My ears _____ long.

3. My tail _____ short and fluffy.

4. My name _____ Flopsy.

5. Carrots _____ my favorite food.

6. Lettuce _____ good for me, too.

7. I _____ a rabbit.

DIRECTIONS → **Write *was* or *were* to finish each sentence.**

8. We _____ tadpoles once.

9. Our mother _____ a big green frog.

10. Our home _____ in the water.

11. We _____ good swimmers.

12. Before long, we _____ frogs like our mother.

Combining Sentences with the Same Subject

Good writers sometimes combine sentences to make their writing more interesting.

Two short sentences might have the same subject. The writer writes the subject once and then combines the two predicates in the same sentence.

Example:

Tara *liked crackers*. Tara *liked cheese*.
Tara liked *crackers and cheese*.

DIRECTIONS → **Combine the predicates in these sentences. Write the new sentences.**

1. Kathy was tired. Kathy wanted her lunch.

_____

_____

2. She turned smoothly in the water. She headed for the other end of the pool.

_____

_____

3. Kathy wanted to win. Kathy hoped to set records.

_____

_____

4. Kathy won many races. Kathy got many awards.

_____

_____

Combining Sentences with the Same Predicate

Good writers often combine short sentences to make their writing more interesting.

Two sentences might have the same predicate. The sentences can be combined by joining the subjects with the word *and*.

Example:

Lance likes to play video games. *Raul* likes to play video games.

Lance and Raul like to play video games.

 **DIRECTIONS** Combine each pair of sentences into one sentence. Remember to join subjects with the word *and*. Write the new sentence.

1. Guppies are pets for fish tanks. Goldfish are pets for fish tanks.

_____

_____

2. Catfish clean harmful moss from the tank. Snails clean harmful moss from the tank.

_____

_____

3. Black mollies are lovely fish. Goldfish are lovely fish.

_____

4. Guppies have live babies. Black mollies have live babies.

_____

5. Zebra fish lay eggs. Angelfish lay eggs.

_____

Joining Sentences

Good writers make their writing more interesting by joining sentences that are short and choppy.

Sentences that have ideas that go together can be joined with a comma (,) and the word *and*.

Example:

The river is beautiful. It is also useful.

The river is beautiful, *and* it is also useful.

DIRECTIONS **Use a comma and the word *and* to join each pair of sentences. Write the new sentence.**

1. Inventions make our lives easier. We take them for granted.

_____

_____

2. We get cold. We turn on a heater.

_____

3. Long ago people got cold. They sat around a fire.

_____

_____

4. A very long time ago, people had no fire. They stayed cold.

_____

_____

5. Our heater works. We stay warm.

_____

Joining Sentences to List Words in a Series

A list of three or more materials or items is called a **series**. Short, choppy sentences can be combined into one long, clear sentence with a series.

Example:

The summer sky *is clear*. The summer sky *is blue*. The summer sky *is beautiful*.

The summer sky *is clear, blue, and beautiful*.

DIRECTIONS → **Join each pair of sentences. Write the new sentence.**

1. Pet mice can be black. They can be red or silver.

_____

2. Other colors for mice include gray. They also include cream and white.

_____

_____

3. A mouse can chew on wood. It can chew on nuts and twigs.

_____

4. Mice clean their own bodies. They clean their faces and ears.

_____

_____

5. Soup cans are good resting places for pet mice. They are good for hamsters and gerbils.

_____

_____

Expanding Sentences

Good writers make sentences clear by using adjectives and adverbs that describe the topic exactly.

Example:

   The blue river rolled lazily through the green land.

DIRECTIONS ▷ **Add an adjective or an adverb where you see this mark: *. The word or words you add should describe the thing or action. Write your new sentences.**

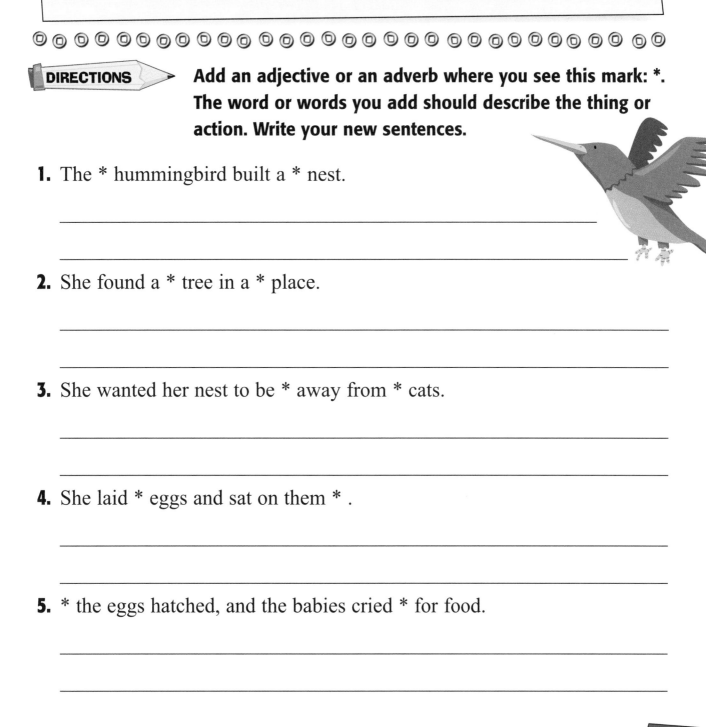

1. The * hummingbird built a * nest.

_____

_____

2. She found a * tree in a * place.

_____

_____

3. She wanted her nest to be * away from * cats.

_____

_____

4. She laid * eggs and sat on them * .

_____

_____

5. * the eggs hatched, and the babies cried * for food.

_____

_____

Avoiding Run-on Sentences

Good writers divide run-on sentences into two or more sentences.
Example:

The sky is blue it is full of clouds.
The sky is blue. It is full of clouds.

DIRECTIONS ▷ **Revise each run-on sentence. Write two shorter sentences to make the meaning clearer.**

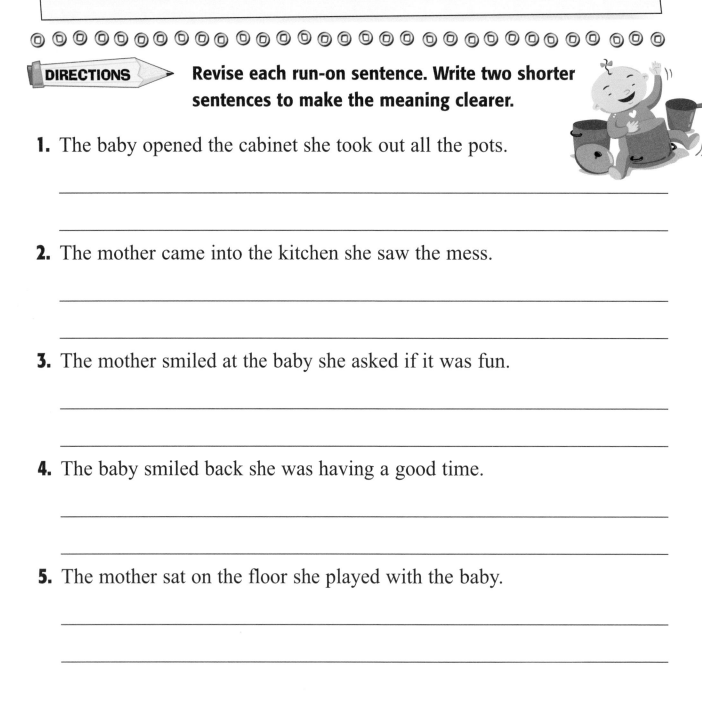

1. The baby opened the cabinet she took out all the pots.

_____

_____

2. The mother came into the kitchen she saw the mess.

_____

_____

3. The mother smiled at the baby she asked if it was fun.

_____

_____

4. The baby smiled back she was having a good time.

_____

_____

5. The mother sat on the floor she played with the baby.

_____

_____

Capital Letters for Names and Titles of People and Pets

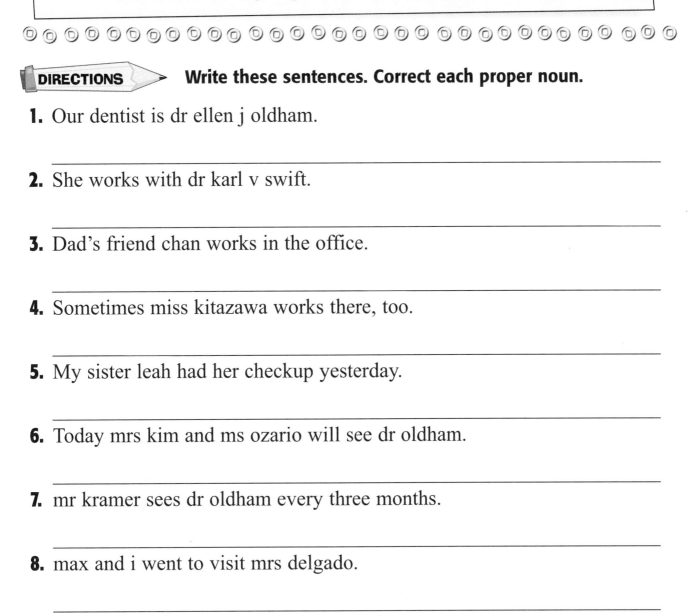

Begin a person's name or a pet's name with a capital letter. Begin titles of a person, such as *Ms.*, *Mr.*, and *Dr.*, with a capital letter. Capitalize initials that take the place of names. Always capitalize the word *I.*

Examples:

   Bob and *I* took my dog *Zak* to see *Dr.* Edward *D.* Porter.

DIRECTIONS > **Write these sentences. Correct each proper noun.**

1. Our dentist is dr ellen j oldham.

_____

2. She works with dr karl v swift.

_____

3. Dad's friend chan works in the office.

_____

4. Sometimes miss kitazawa works there, too.

_____

5. My sister leah had her checkup yesterday.

_____

6. Today mrs kim and ms ozario will see dr oldham.

_____

7. mr kramer sees dr oldham every three months.

_____

8. max and i went to visit mrs delgado.

_____

Capital Letters for Place Names

Begin the name of a town, city, state, and country with a capital letter.
Begin the name of a street and its abbreviation with a capital letter.
Examples:

   Akron, Ohio   Mexico   Jones Road

DIRECTIONS ▸ **Write each place name correctly.**

1. zion national park _____

2. state street _____

3. south america _____

4. mississippi river _____

5. handy hardware store _____

DIRECTIONS ▸ **Change each sentence. Use a place name for the underlined words. Write your new sentences.**

6. Ms. Bass lived in <u>a city</u>.

_____

7. She was a teacher at <u>a school</u>.

_____

8. She lived in a building on <u>a street</u>.

_____

9. One summer she visited <u>a state</u>.

_____

10. Pierre lived in <u>a foreign country</u>.

_____

Capital Letters for Days, Months, and Holidays

Begin the name of a day, month, or holiday with a capital letter.

Examples:

Wednesday

January

New Year's Day

January

Sun	Mon	Tues	Wed	Thur	Fri	Sat
			1	2	3	4
5	6	7	8	9	10	11
12	13	14	15	16	17	18
19	20	21	22	23	24	25
26	27	28	29	30	31	

DIRECTIONS ▸ **Write each day, month, or holiday correctly.**

1. february _____

2. monday _____

3. labor day_____

4. november _____

5. saturday _____

6. thanksgiving day _____

DIRECTIONS ▸ **Finish each sentence. Write the name of a day, a month, or a holiday. Be sure to begin the name with a capital letter.**

7. I think _____ is a good day to play outside.

8. For me, _____ is the best school day.

9. _____ is often a day when everything seems to go wrong.

10. I think the best month of the year is _____.

11. _____ is the month of my birthday.

12. _____ is a great month for swimming.

Using Capital Letters

A proper noun names a special person, place, or thing. It begins with a capital letter.

Example:

Pompeii was an ancient city.

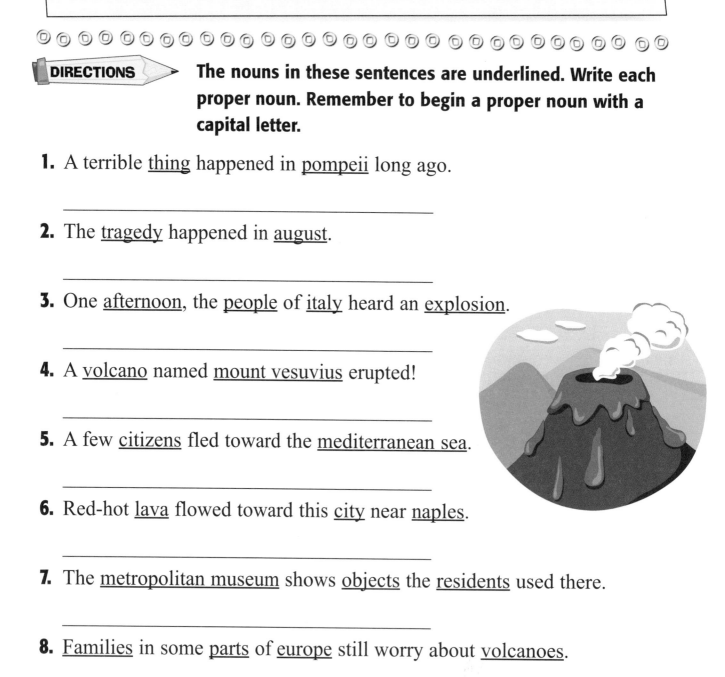

DIRECTIONS ▷ **The nouns in these sentences are underlined. Write each proper noun. Remember to begin a proper noun with a capital letter.**

1. A terrible <u>thing</u> happened in <u>pompeii</u> long ago.

_____

2. The <u>tragedy</u> happened in <u>august</u>.

_____

3. One <u>afternoon</u>, the <u>people</u> of <u>italy</u> heard an <u>explosion</u>.

_____

4. A <u>volcano</u> named <u>mount vesuvius</u> erupted!

_____

5. A few <u>citizens</u> fled toward the <u>mediterranean sea</u>.

_____

6. Red-hot <u>lava</u> flowed toward this <u>city</u> near <u>naples</u>.

_____

7. The <u>metropolitan museum</u> shows <u>objects</u> the <u>residents</u> used there.

_____

8. <u>Families</u> in some <u>parts</u> of <u>europe</u> still worry about <u>volcanoes</u>.

_____

Periods

Use a **period (.)** at the end of a statement or a command.
Use a period after an abbreviation.
Use a period after a numeral in the main topic of an outline.
Examples:

Manny and Tony like the beach.
Mr. Smith swims in the summer.

Wind Power
I. Using wind power on the sea
II. Using wind power on land

DIRECTIONS ▶ **Read each sentence. Add periods where they are needed.**

1. Manny and Tony go to the beach every day
2. Do not step on the crabs
3. Dr Quick looked at Mr Smith's toe.
4. Mrs Smith found a bandage
5. Dr Quick helped Mr Smith.

DIRECTIONS ▶ **Add periods to the outline where they are needed.**

Beach Activities
I Play in the waves
II Look for shells
III Have a picnic

Abbreviations and Initials

An **abbreviation** is a short way of writing a word or words.
Use capital letters and periods to write most abbreviations.
An **initial** is an abbreviation of a name. The initial is the first letter of the name.
Use capital letters and periods to write an initial.
Examples:

Doctor = *Dr.*   Street = *St.*

Monday = *Mon.*   October = *Oct.*

DIRECTIONS ➤ **Write the following items. Use abbreviations or initials wherever possible. Use capital letters correctly.**

1. circle road _____

2. july _____

3. doctor Homer amos mancebo

_____

4. tuesday _____

5. 493 dinosaur avenue

_____

6. Mister willard Ambrose

_____

7. saturday, april 13

_____

8. angela phyllis mills

_____

DIRECTIONS ➤ **Each of these items has at least one error. Correct the item, and write it on the line.**

9. mon _____

10. Miss Cynthia a forbes

_____

11. feb. 28 _____

12. deerpath rd.

_____

Commas in Sentences

Use a **comma (,)** after *yes*, *no*, and *well* at the beginning of a sentence.
Use a comma before the word *and* when two sentences are joined.
Examples:

Well, that was a strange place.
Yes, it was scary, *and* I don't want to go back.

DIRECTIONS ▶ **Write a sentence to answer each question. Begin each sentence with *Yes*, *No*, or *Well*.**

1. Did you ever give a dog a bath?

_____

2. What do you need in order to give a dog a bath?

_____

_____

3. Would you like to give a dog a bath this afternoon?

_____

_____

4. Do you have a favorite book?

_____

5. What is that funny animal?

_____

6. Is the big game on Friday?

_____

Commas in a Series

Use a **comma (,)** after each item except the last one in a series of three or more items.
Examples:

The desert is *hot, dry, and sandy.*
Snakes, lizards, and tortoises live there.

DIRECTIONS → **Rewrite each sentence. Add commas where they belong.**

1. An octopus has eight legs large eyes and strong jaws.

_____

_____

2. An octopus eats clams crabs and lobsters.

_____

3. Octopuses live along the coasts of Hawaii Australia and China.

_____

_____

4. The desert seems to shimmer shine and bubble in the hot sun.

_____

_____

5. Sometimes the wind will blow swirl or whip the sand around.

_____

_____

More Uses for Commas

Use a **comma (,)** between a city and a state or a city and a country.
Use a comma between the day and the year.
Use a comma after the greeting in a friendly letter and after the closing of any letter.
Examples:

Topeka, Kansas   Osaka, Japan
September 17, 2005
Dear Mr. Wong,   Your friend,

 **DIRECTIONS** **Read this friendly letter. Add commas where they are needed.**

New Delhi India

May 3 2005

Dear Chandra

Today I watched the sun rise from beside the river in our city. As I watched the sun, a beautiful paper boat floated toward the shore. I caught the boat and read your name and address. The shiuli flowers were still fresh. They reminded me of the beauty of the morning. Thank you for sending your boat. It helped me to appreciate the new day and reminded me of forgotten dreams.

May your boats find many new friends for you.

Sincerely

Sadar Rangairi

Colons and Apostrophes

Use a **colon (:)** between the hour and the minute in the time of day.
Use an **apostrophe (')** to show that one or more letters have been left out in a contraction.
Add an apostrophe and an *s* to singular nouns to show possession.
Add an apostrophe to plural nouns that end in *s* to show possession.
Examples:

    1:15 PM   6:30 AM

    is not = *isn't*   have not = *haven't*

    Amelia's project   the *cat's* whiskers

    girls' laughter   *parents'* plan

DIRECTIONS ➤ **Complete each sentence correctly. Add colons and apostrophes where they are needed.**

1. Meghan and her family took the 8 30 PM train.

2. At 7 15 the next morning, they ate breakfast.

3. The train pulled into Union Station at 8 45 AM.

4. Meghan didn t want to waste time.

5. She wasn t interested in looking at the city from their windows.

6. Meghan s cousins met them at the hotel.

7. Her cousins rooms overlooked the lake.

8. Meghan s father took them to the fair.

9. They stayed at the fair until 9 00 PM.

10. Meghan couldn t stay awake on the ride home.

Contractions with *Not*

A **contraction** is a short way of writing two words together. Some of the letters are left out. An apostrophe takes the place of the missing letters.
Use verbs and the word *not* to form some contractions.
Examples:

were + not = *weren't*   have + not = *haven't*
will + not = *won't*   could + not = *couldn't*

DIRECTIONS ▷ **Finish each sentence. Write the contraction of the word or words in ( ).**

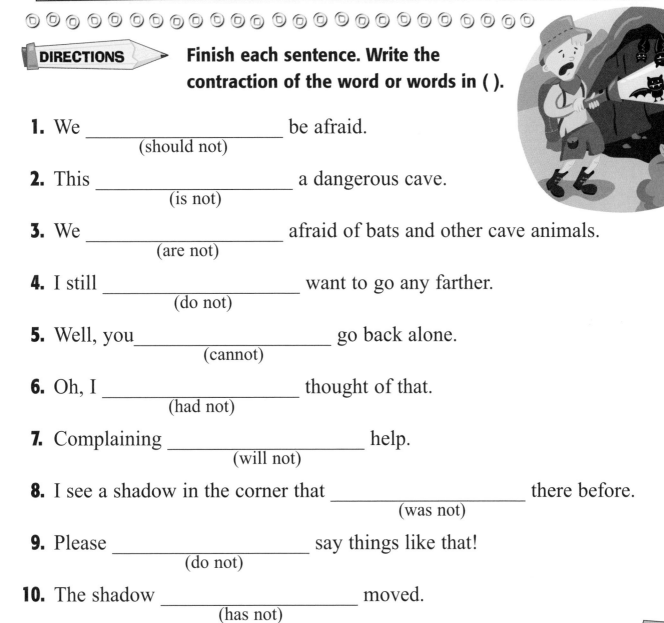

1. We _____ be afraid.
   (should not)

2. This _____ a dangerous cave.
   (is not)

3. We _____ afraid of bats and other cave animals.
   (are not)

4. I still _____ want to go any farther.
   (do not)

5. Well, you_____ go back alone.
   (cannot)

6. Oh, I _____ thought of that.
   (had not)

7. Complaining _____ help.
   (will not)

8. I see a shadow in the corner that _____ there before.
   (was not)

9. Please _____ say things like that!
   (do not)

10. The shadow _____ moved.
    (has not)

75

Direct Quotations and Dialogue

Use **quotation marks (" ")** before and after the words a speaker says.
Begin the first word a speaker says with a capital letter.
Examples:

Sam asked, "Where did you go?"

"I went fishing," Ed said.

DIRECTIONS ➤ **Read each sentence. If it is correct, write *correct*. If it needs quotation marks and a capital letter, write the sentence correctly.**

1. Lily said, let's go to the beach.

_____

2. Jeff exclaimed, that's a great idea!

_____

3. Dad said that he would rather stay home.

_____

4. Uncle Bill said, well, I'd love to go to the beach.

_____

5. Jeff asked, where is our big beach ball?

_____

6. Uncle Bill said that he would pack a picnic lunch.

_____

7. Dad reminded them, don't forget your towels.

_____

8. Lily shouted, this is great!

_____

Titles

Begin the first word, last word, and all other important words in a title with a capital letter.
Underline the title of a book.
Use quotation marks to write the title of a story, a poem, or a song.
Examples:

<u>The Magic Windmill</u> (book)
"Wind in the Orchard" (story)
"Capture the Wind" (poem)

 **DIRECTIONS** **Write each sentence correctly. Add underlines, quotation marks, and capital letters where they are needed.**

1. Chet got a book called the story of baseball from the library today.

_____

_____

2. The first story, titled in the beginning, starts in 1846.

_____

_____

3. The last story is called why is baseball so popular?

_____

_____

4. Last week Chet read a book called pioneers of baseball by Robert Smith.

_____

_____

5. His favorite story, the one and only, is about Babe Ruth.

_____

Compound Words

A **compound word** is formed by putting together two smaller words. The first word in a compound word usually describes the second.

Examples:

black + berry = *blackberry*
bed + room = *bedroom*

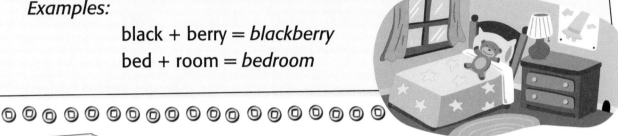

DIRECTIONS ➤ **Circle the compound word in each sentence. Then, write the two words that form the compound word, and write the meaning of the compound word.**

1. "Let's play an outdoor game," said Penny.

_____

2. "The playground is open," said Paul, "so let's go there."

_____

3. "Maybe you should wear an overcoat," said Penny's mom.

_____

4. "A lightweight jacket is all I need," said Penny.

_____

5. "All right, but be back by mealtime," said Penny's mom.

_____

6. "It's a beautiful afternoon," said Paul.

_____

7. "Even the mockingbird in that tree likes it," Paul declared.

_____

8. "Look at the pretty leaves in the treetop," said Penny.

_____

Synonyms

A **synonym** is a word that has almost the same meaning as another word.

Examples:

   Afraid is a synonym of *scared.*

   Begin is a synonym of *start.*

 **DIRECTIONS** Read each sentence. Choose the word in ( ) that is a synonym for each underlined word. Then, rewrite the sentence using the synonym.

1. The pyramids of Egypt have stood for <u>almost</u> 5,000 years. (nearly, over, exactly)

_____

_____

2. Because the pyramids are so <u>huge</u>, strong, and old, people find them interesting. (small, heavy, large)

_____

_____

3. To <u>understand</u> anything about the pyramids, we have to learn about Egypt of that time. (write, forget, know)

_____

_____

4. The rulers of ancient Egypt ruled over a <u>complete</u> country, not just a town or a tribe. (whole, small, growing)

_____

_____

Antonyms

An **antonym** is a word that means the opposite of another word.
Examples:
> *Up* is an antonym of *down.*
> *Fast* is an antonym of *slow.*

 **DIRECTIONS** ➤ **Read each pair of sentences. Find two antonyms and write them on the line.**

1. Getting started with soap carving is the hardest part. The easiest thing is to talk about it.

_____

2. Do not cut soap toward yourself. It is best to cut slowly away from yourself.

_____

3. Keep your knife clean. A dirty blade is hard to use.

_____

4. Remember to keep your soap dry. Don't forget that soap and water make soap suds.

_____

5. If you paint the soap, it is a good idea to test a small part. If it looks bad, try a different color.

_____

6. A fresh cake of soap is best. An old cake of soap might be partly dried out.

_____

7. A small cake of soap is very difficult to work with. It's best to use a large piece.

_____

Prefixes

A **prefix** is a letter or group of letters added to the beginning of a base word. A prefix changes the meaning of a word.
Examples:

I *agree* that the pet needs a name.

I *disagree* with your ideas for names.

Prefix	Meaning	Example
dis	not	<u>dis</u>like
im	not	<u>im</u>possible
re	again	<u>re</u>do
re	back	<u>re</u>pay
un	not	<u>un</u>lucky
un	opposite of	<u>un</u>wrap

 **DIRECTIONS** → **Read each sentence. Change the meaning of each sentence by adding a prefix from the list above to each underlined word. Rewrite the sentence using the new word.**

1. Lexi was a very <u>usual</u> animal.

_____

2. She was <u>patient</u> to get out into the world.

_____

3. Lexi <u>liked</u> the pet store.

_____

4. Every night she felt <u>lucky</u> to be there.

_____

5. Lexi thought it was <u>possible</u> to find a new home.

_____

Suffixes

A **suffix** is a letter or group of letters added to the end of a base word. A suffix changes the meaning of a word.

Examples:

Amelia made the roller coaster work<u>able</u>.

She was a very good thin<u>ker</u>.

Suffix	Meaning	Example
able	able to be	wear<u>able</u>
er	one who	build<u>er</u>
ful	full of	hope<u>ful</u>
ible	able to be	flex<u>ible</u>
less	without	care<u>less</u>
or	one who	visit<u>or</u>

DIRECTIONS ➤ **Read each sentence. Choose a suffix from the above list to write a single word that has the same meaning as the words in ( ). Write the new word on the line.**

1. When Amelia Earhart was a girl, she was the (person who invents) of a roller coaster. _____

2. It was a (full of use) ride. _____

3. Her sister Muriel was her (person who helps). _____

4. Amelia was (without fear) and rode on it. _____

5. She felt (full of joy) as she flew down. _____

6. Her first (full of success) ride ended at her grandmother's feet.

_____

Homographs

Homographs are words that have the same spelling but different meanings.
Some homographs are pronounced differently.
Examples:
> *felt*: a soft kind of cloth
> *felt*: sensed something on the skin
> *wind*: moving air
> *wind*: to turn a knob on something

ⓞ ⓞ

 **DIRECTIONS** ➤ **Read each sentence. Circle the correct meaning of the underlined word.**

1. While Buddy counted to 20, Buster ran to <u>hide</u>.
   a. get out of sight
   b. the skin of an animal

2. Buddy looked all <u>over</u>, but he couldn't find Buster.
   a. finished, done
   b. around

3. After a <u>long</u> time, Buddy gave up.
   a. to want something very much
   b. lot of

4. "Come out!" shouted Buddy, but Buster stayed under the <u>house</u>.
   a. a building where people live
   b. an audience

5. Buddy began to worry because the weather was <u>turning</u> cold.
   a. changing
   b. spinning

6. It felt like <u>fall</u>.
   a. a tumble to the ground
   b. autumn

DIRECTIONS ➤ **Read the sentence. Then, write another sentence using the underlined word as a noun.**

7. "Don't <u>throw</u> the ball so hard!" said Buster.

Homophones

Homophones are words that sound alike but are spelled differently and have different meanings.
Example:

A *pair* of girls sat at the table.
They were sharing a *pear*.

DIRECTIONS Read each sentence. Choose the homophone in ( ) that correctly completes it. Circle the correct homophone.

1. For seven (daze, days), Julie has been trying to bake a good fruit pie.

2. She has three (pears, pairs) and three apples.

3. She will have to sift the (flower, flour) for the crust.

4. She can never (seam, seem) to get the crust right.

5. The (dough, doe) is always just a little too dry.

6. This is day number (ate, eight).

7. Jan and (I, eye) are hoping this one is good.

8. If Julie gets it (write, right) this time, we will be happy for her.

9. I tasted a (piece, peace) of Julie's first pie.

10. That time it was (fare, fair), but not really excellent.

DIRECTIONS Underline the pair of homophones in each sentence.

11. One time Julie won a cooking contest.

12. Twice in the past year, the judges passed over her dishes.

13. Did you ever find a cook who was fined for bad cooking?

Troublesome Words: *to, too, two*

Use *to* when you mean "in the direction of."
Use *too* when you mean "also."
Use *two* when you mean the number 2.
Examples:

      I am going *to* a movie.
      My friends are going, *too*.
      Each ticket costs *two* dollars.

DIRECTIONS   **Complete each sentence correctly by writing *to*, *too*, or *two*.**

1. We went _____ the theater.

2. The mayor came, _____.

3. An usher showed us _____ our seats.

4. "Welcome _____ the best show ever!" an announcer said.

5. The first _____ performers did a number of good tricks.

6. They sang songs, _____.

7. Then, _____ actors told some funny jokes.

8. I had never been _____ a vaudeville show before.

9. There were _____ songs in the finale.

10. "I know this song and the last one, _____," the mayor said.

Troublesome Words: *its*, *it's*

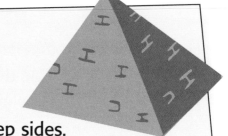

Use *its* when you mean "belonging to it."
Use *it's* when you mean "it is."
Examples:
> The pyramid is huge. We climbed *its* steep sides.
> *It's* fun to explore.

DIRECTIONS Use *its* or *it's* to complete each sentence. Write the correct word on the line.

1. What is that? _____ a mummy!

2. _____ thousands of years old.

3. _____ wrapped tightly in strips of cloth.

4. The inner chamber of the pyramid is large. Ancient drawings cover _____ walls.

5. In one picture, a dog follows _____ owner.

6. _____ teeth are long and sharp.

7. Look at this mask. _____ made of solid gold!

8. _____ important to keep careful records.

9. Photograph each item, and write down _____ exact location.

10. _____ a job that is certain to take many weeks.

Troublesome Words: *your, you're*

Use *your* when you mean "belonging to you."
Use *you're* when you mean "you are."
Examples:
> Do you have *your* homework?
> *You're* in trouble now.

DIRECTIONS Use *your* or *you're* to complete each sentence.
Write the correct word on the line.

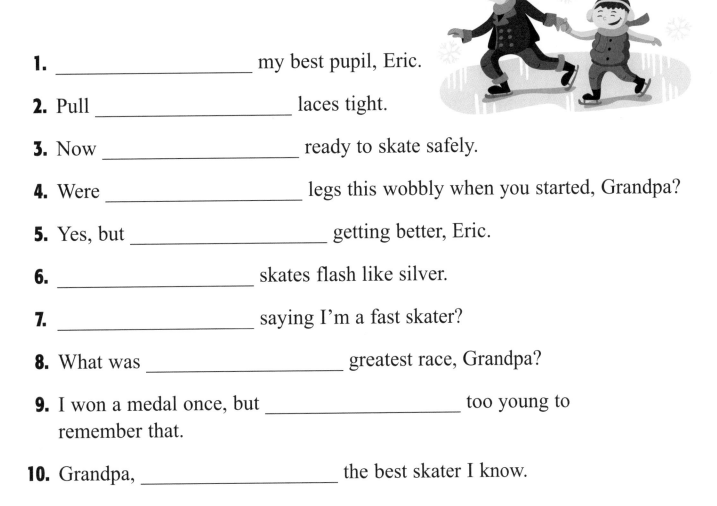

1. _____ my best pupil, Eric.

2. Pull _____ laces tight.

3. Now _____ ready to skate safely.

4. Were _____ legs this wobbly when you started, Grandpa?

5. Yes, but _____ getting better, Eric.

6. _____ skates flash like silver.

7. _____ saying I'm a fast skater?

8. What was _____ greatest race, Grandpa?

9. I won a medal once, but _____ too young to remember that.

10. Grandpa, _____ the best skater I know.

Troublesome Words:
their, there, they're

Use *their* when you mean "belonging to them."
Use *there* to tell where.
Use *they're* when you mean "they are."
Examples:
    Pirates sailed in *their* ships.
    The captain hid his jewels over *there*.
    They're beautiful jewels!

DIRECTIONS → Use *their*, *there*, or *they're* to complete each sentence. Write the correct word on the line.

1. Liz and Han are working on _____ new computer program.

2. _____ staying after school today.

3. _____ going to be in the computer lab.

4. They can use one of the computers _____.

5. They might be able to ask _____ teacher some questions.

6. She's often _____, too.

7. Today she can't answer _____ questions.

8. "Maybe you'd like to talk with the teachers sitting over _____," she says.

9. "_____ talking about computers."

10. Han and Liz ask the teachers _____ questions.

Using Sensory Words

Good writers use sensory words to tell how someone or something looks, feels, sounds, smells, or tastes.
Examples:
      The old coin was *shiny* and *bright*.
      The cat's fur was *soft* and *smooth*.

DIRECTIONS ▶ **Read each sentence. Decide which one of the senses is being used. Write *look*, *feel*, *sound*, *taste*, or *smell* on the line.**

1. The chimneys were outlined against a pale, pink sky.

_____

2. The morning air was very chilly. _____

3. Suddenly, a loud cry broke the silence. _____

4. A young boy poked his head out of one chimney.

_____

5. The boy called "All up!" in a loud voice. _____

6. He waved his cleaning tools. _____

7. Then he slid into the chimney to clean it. _____

8. Later he had some spicy cider to drink. _____

9. He warmed his hands on the hot cup. _____

10. The smell of roast pork filled the air. _____

Choosing Words to Paint a Vivid Picture

Good writers choose words that paint a vivid picture. Sometimes, writers compare two things so that you can understand one of them better.
Examples:
    Paul Bunyan was as big as *a tree*.
    His feet smelled like *dead fish*.

DIRECTIONS > Read each word picture. Underline the two things that are being compared. Then, tell how they are alike.

1. The fog comes in like a cat.

_____

2. The fog covered the top of the hill like a blanket.

_____

3. The tree, like an umbrella, protected us from the rain.

_____

4. The moon smiled down on us, just as Grandma always did.

_____

5. The light reflected off the lake as if the lake were a mirror.

_____

6. The grasshoppers called back and forth to each other like an echo in the mountains.

_____

7. Like a knife through butter, the boat went through the water.

_____

Subject and Verb Agreement

A subject and its verb must agree in number.
To make most verbs agree with singular subjects, add *s*.
To make verbs that end in *sh*, *ch*, *ss*, or *x* agree with singular subjects, add *es*.
To make most verbs agree with plural subjects, do not change the ending.
Examples:

> She *walks* along a sandy trail.
> The *rain washes* the flowers of the cacti.
> The *birds sing* after it rains.

 **DIRECTIONS** → **Read each sentence. Circle the form of the verb that agrees with the subject of the sentence.**

1. The girl (stroll, strolls) with her grandmother.

2. The girl (watch, watches) everything around her.

3. She (enjoy, enjoys) the quail most.

4. Five quail (pass, passes) in front of her.

5. The girl (see, sees) quail eggs in a nest.

6. They (touch, touches) none of them.

7. Grandmother (take, takes) water from the cacti.

8. They (fill, fills) their basket with fruit.

9. Grandmother (teach, teaches) the girl about the desert.

10. The girl (understand, understands) how beautiful it is.

More Subject and Verb Agreement

Remember that a subject and its verb must agree in number.
A singular subject must have a singular verb.
A plural subject must have a plural verb.
Examples:
My *frog is* green.
Frogs live both on land and in water.

DIRECTIONS ➤ **Read each pair of sentences. On the line, write a verb that would make sense.**

1. Emilio's yard has a garden and a creek. He _____ outside all day.

2. The garden needs water to grow. Emilio _____ the garden.

3. Emilio's grandfather plants flowers there. They _____ quickly.

4. Frogs in the creek croak loudly. Emilio _____ them in the evening.

5. Tadpoles are young frogs. They _____ in the water, just like fish.

6. One day Emilio finds a rabbit's nest. The mother rabbit _____ in front of him.

7. Emilio wonders how many baby rabbits are in the nest. He _____ eight of them.

8. Emilio knows the mother will come right back. He _____ away from the nest.

Paragraphs

A **paragraph** is a group of sentences that tells about one main idea. The first line of a paragraph is indented. This means the first word is moved in a little from the left margin.

The **topic sentence** tells the main idea of the paragraph.

The other sentences in a paragraph are the **detail sentences**. Detail sentences tell about the main idea.

Example:

Hunter spiders hunt for their food. Some hunters use their teeth to catch food. Other hunters run to trap food. Some jump on insects to catch them.

How to Write a Paragraph

1. Write a topic sentence that clearly tells the main idea of your paragraph.
2. Indent the first line.
3. Write detail sentences that tell about the main idea.

DIRECTIONS → **Read the example paragraph. List three details that tell about the main idea.**

_____

_____

_____

_____

_____

_____

Using Enough Details

Good writers give readers interesting details and clear examples.
Be sure to use enough details to support your main idea.

DIRECTIONS ➤ **Read each paragraph. Answer the questions.**

Owls are best known for their ability to see at night. They can see 100 times better than humans. Their eyes are big and do not move very easily. This is why owls' necks have to turn so far.

Though they can also see well in the daytime, owls are known for seeing at night. They can see 100 times better at night than humans can, but they are color-blind. Owls' eyes are very large, and they control the light coming in by changing the size of the pupils of the eyes. Each pupil acts alone. If you stood in the sunlight and your friend stood in the shade, an owl could see each of you well.

1. Which paragraph is more interesting? Explain your answer.

_____

_____

2. What is the topic sentence of the second paragraph?

_____

_____

3. What is one detail given in the second paragraph?

_____

_____

4. Write one example found in the second paragraph.

_____

_____

Keeping to the Topic

A good writer plans a paragraph so that it gives details about one main idea.

All the sentences in a paragraph must keep to the topic.

◎◎◎◎◎◎◎◎◎◎◎◎◎◎◎◎◎◎◎◎◎◎◎◎◎◎◎◎◎◎◎◎◎◎◎◎◎

DIRECTIONS ▷ **Read the underlined topic sentence below. Choose the sentences that keep to the topic. Write a paragraph, using the topic sentence and the sentences you chose.**

<u>A sighted person can imagine what it is like to be blind.</u>
Put a scarf over your eyes to block out light.
Try to figure out what different foods are.
Being deaf is not easy, either.
Pretend to pay for something with coins.
Try to walk into another room and sit at a table.
A person who cannot hear has different problems.
Blind people can do all these things and more.

_____

_____

_____

_____

_____

_____

_____

_____

_____

Personal Narrative

In a **personal narrative**, a writer tells about an experience in his or her life.

Example:

> Why was I named Cameroon Pele? I never thought about it until a friend asked how I got my name. I didn't know, so I went home to search for answers. First, I sat down to think. Then my sister Helen came in. She was born on the day a volcano named Mount St. Helens erupted. That's how she got her name. I asked her how I had gotten mine. She said that I got my name the same way she did. It's true. I looked it up. I was born on the same day a volcano erupted in Cameroon, Africa.

How to Write a Paragraph That Tells about Yourself

1. Tell about yourself. Use the pronouns *I*, *me*, and *my* to tell about yourself.
2. Write about events in order. Use time-order words.
3. Your narrative should have a beginning, middle, and end.
4. The beginning should introduce the experience.
5. The middle should describe the events in time order.
6. The ending should bring the experience to a close.

Personal Narrative, page 2

 **DIRECTIONS** ▷ **Read the example paragraph on page 96. Then, answer the questions.**

1. Why did the writer write this story?

_____

_____

2. How do you know this is a personal narrative?

_____

_____

3. What is the writer's problem?

_____

_____

DIRECTIONS ▷ **Think about something that has happened to you. Use the graphic organizer to plan your personal narrative.**

WRITING PLAN

Beginning	Name the experience you will write about:
Middle	Name three things that happened in the experience:
Ending	Tell how the experience turned out:

Tips for Writing a Personal Narrative:
- Write from your point of view. Use the words *I, me,* and *my* to show your reader that this is your story.
- Think about what you want to tell your reader.
- Organize your ideas into a beginning, middle, and end.
- Write an interesting introduction that "grabs" your reader.
- Write an ending for your story. Tell how the experience ended.

> **DIRECTIONS**

Think about something that has happened to you. Tell about what happened to you in a paragraph. Write at least three sentences. Use your writing plan from page 97 as a guide for writing your personal narrative.

_____

_____

_____

_____

_____

_____

_____

_____

_____

_____

_____

Poem

In a **poem**, a writer paints a picture with words. Poems often describe something in an unusual or interesting way. Many poems also have rhyming words. The words in a poem often have a definite rhythm, or beat.

Examples:

Rhymed Poem

Cat and Mouse

The mouse poked out her tiny head.
"Look and listen," her mother said.
She heard a bell, and that was that.
The clever mouse escaped the cat.

Unrhymed Poem

Not all poems rhyme. Read how the poem might be written without rhyme.

Cat and Mouse

Like a guard watching for danger,
the mouse peeked around for the cat.

Like an alarm ringing out a warning,
the cat's bell signaled the mouse.

As quick as an eye blink,
the mouse disappeared.

How to Write a Poem

1. Choose a topic for your poem.
2. Give your poem a title.
3. Use colorful words to paint a picture.
4. If you want, use rhyme and rhythm to help you express feelings.

Poem, page 2

1. Which of the two poems do you like better? Explain why.

   _____

   _____

   _____

2. What are the rhyming words in the first poem?

   _____

   _____

3. Read the third and fourth lines of the second poem. What is the cat's bell compared to?

   _____

   _____

DIRECTIONS ▷ Finish the poem below. Think of colorful words and words that rhyme. Write another verse for the poem. Then, make up a title for it.

_____

The frog wants a drink.
He hops into the sink.

The _____ water comes down.

Will the _____ frog _____?

_____

_____

_____

Poem, page 3

Tips for Writing a Poem:
- Choose a topic for your poem.
- Use colorful words to paint a picture for your reader.
- Use rhythm and rhyme to express your feelings.
- Use words that begin with the same sound.
- Use words that imitate sounds.
- Make comparisons between things that do not seem alike.
- Give your poem a title.

DIRECTIONS → **Think about something that you like to do. Then, think of colorful words that describe it. Use the words in a poem. Write at least eight lines.**

_____

_____

_____

_____

_____

_____

_____

_____

Descriptive Paragraph

In a **descriptive paragraph**, a writer describes a person, place, thing, or event.

A good description lets the reader see, feel, hear, and sometimes taste or smell what is being described.

Example:

Last fall, the air was crisp and cool as Alberto and his big brother waited for the parade to pass. Suddenly, they heard the thump of the big school drum. The parade was coming! Alberto was tall, but even he had trouble seeing over all the people. Beside Alberto, a little girl with a sweet-smelling jelly doughnut was crying. She couldn't see a thing. Alberto lifted the little girl to his shoulders. Then she could see all the high-stepping marchers. The little girl squealed with delight!

How to Write a Descriptive Paragraph

1. Write a topic sentence that clearly tells what the paragraph is about.
2. Add detail sentences. Use colorful words to give information about your topic.
3. Make an exact picture for the reader with the words you choose.

Descriptive Paragraph, page 2

DIRECTIONS ⟩ **Read the example description on page 102. Then, answer the questions.**

1. In what season does the parade take place? _____

2. What are some words the writer uses that appeal to your senses?

_____

_____

3. What are some descriptions the writer uses to help you imagine what is happening in the story?

_____

_____

_____

DIRECTIONS ⟩ **Think about something that you would like to describe. It could be a thing, a person you know, or something that has happened to you. Write it in the circle. Then, write words that describe your topic on the lines below. Use the graphic organizer to plan your descriptive paragraph.**

WRITING PLAN

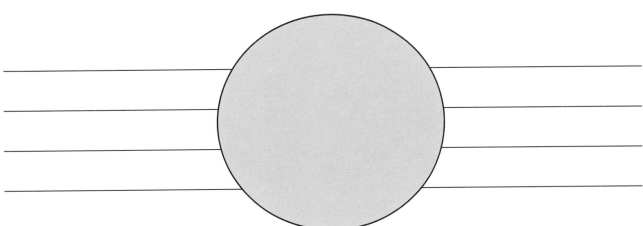

Descriptive Paragraph, page 3

Tips for Writing a Descriptive Paragraph:

- Describe a person, a place, an object, or an event.
- Paint a picture using words.
- Use words that appeal to the reader's senses. Let the reader see, smell, taste, feel, and hear what you are writing about.
- Include a sentence that introduces your topic.
- Write detail sentences that use descriptive words.

DIRECTIONS **Think about something that you would like to describe. Introduce your topic in your first sentence. Then, use the words that you wrote in the graphic organizer on page 103 to describe it. Be sure to appeal to the reader's senses.**

Friendly Letter

A person writes to someone he or she knows in a **friendly letter**. A friendly letter has five parts: a heading, a greeting, a body, a closing, and a signature.

Example:

heading ——— 27 Green Street
Burlington, NC 27215
April 10, 2005

greeting — Dear Grandma,

body —   Sandy and I are fine. Last night he was a busy hamster. He rearranged the wood shavings in his habitat. I love watching him. Please give Aunt Jenny a hug and a kiss for me.

closing ——— Love,

signature ——— Mimi

How to Write a Friendly Letter

1. In the heading, include a comma between the name of the city and state and between the day of the month and the year.
2. End the greeting with a comma.
3. Write a friendly message in the body.
4. End the closing with a comma.
5. Sign the letter with your name.

Friendly Letter, page 2

DIRECTIONS → **Read the example friendly letter on page 105. Then, answer the questions.**

1. Who wrote this letter? _____

2. What is the writer's address?

_____

_____

3. What is the greeting of this letter? _____

4. What is the writer writing about in this letter?

_____

Address an Envelope

An envelope is used to send a letter or a note.
The receiver's address goes toward the center.
The return address is in the upper left corner.
Postal abbreviations are used for state names.
The ZIP Code goes after the state abbreviation.
Example:

Geraldine Roberts
8 Maple Drive
Camp Hill, PA 17011 — **return address**   **stamp**

Wendy Garrison
220 Arlington Ave.   **receiver's name and address**
Bolivar, NY 14715

Friendly Letter, page 3

Tips for Writing a Friendly Letter:
- Think of someone to write to.
- Think of something to write about.
- Write your friendly letter.
- Be sure to include all the parts.
- Fill out the envelope correctly.

heading _____

_____

_____

greeting _____

body _____

_____

_____

_____

_____

_____

_____

closing _____

signature _____

How-to Paragraph

A **how-to paragraph** gives directions or explains how to do something. Steps are given in time order.
Example:

How to Make a Volcano

You can make a small volcano at home with an adult's help. You will need a pan, a plastic bottle, red food coloring, a bottle of vinegar, baking soda, and some sand. First, add a few drops of food coloring to the vinegar. Next, fill the plastic bottle halfway with baking soda and place it in the middle of the pan. Pile the sand around the bottle. Finally, have an adult quickly pour the vinegar into the hole. Stand back, and let the volcano erupt.

How to Write a How-to Paragraph

1. Write a topic sentence that tells what you are going to explain.
2. Add a detail sentence that tells what materials are needed.
3. Write detail sentences that tell the steps in the directions.
4. Use time-order words such as *first*, *next*, *then*, and *finally* to show correct order.

How-to Paragraph, page 2

DIRECTIONS ▷ **Read the example how-to paragraph on page 108. Then, answer the questions.**

1. What does this paragraph tell you how to do? _____

_____

2. What materials are needed to make this thing?

_____

_____

3. What is the first step?

_____

4. What time-order words does the writer use?

_____

DIRECTIONS ▷ **Think about something you want to tell others how to do. Use this writing plan to help you.**

WRITING PLAN

1. What will you tell others how to do?

2. What materials are needed?

3. What steps must the reader follow? Number the steps.

4. What time-order words will you use?

How-to Paragraph, page 3

DIRECTIONS Think about something you want to tell others how to do. Use your writing plan from page 109 as a guide for writing your how-to paragraph.

_____

_____

_____

_____

_____

_____

_____

_____

_____

_____

_____

_____

_____

_____

_____

Information Paragraph

An **information paragraph** gives facts about one topic. It has a topic sentence that tells the main idea. At least two detail sentences give facts about the main idea.

Example:

The Peak of Perfection

    Mount Cameroon is a special mountain in Africa. It is the highest mountain in western Africa and an active volcano. The last time Mount Cameroon erupted was more than 30 years ago. Ash that came out of the volcano turned into rich soil. Farmers now grow tea, rubber trees, and cocoa in that soil. Mount Cameroon is also special because it is one of the wettest places on earth. More than 400 inches of rain fall there each year.

title

topic
sentence

detail
sentences

How to Write an Information Paragraph
1. Write a topic sentence that tells your main idea.
2. Write detail sentences that give information about your main idea.
3. Think of a title for your information paragraph.

Information Paragraph, page 2

 **DIRECTIONS** > **Read the example information paragraph on page 111. Then, answer the questions.**

1. What is the main idea of the information paragraph?

_____

_____

2. When did Mount Cameroon last erupt? _____

3. Write one detail sentence from the paragraph.

_____

_____

_____

 **DIRECTIONS** > **Think about a topic you would like to write about. Use this writing plan to help you.**

WRITING PLAN

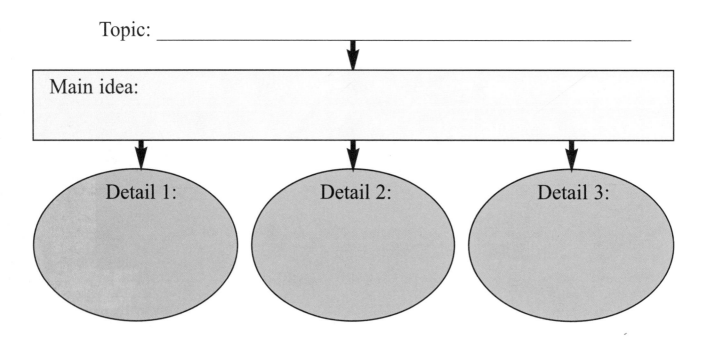

Topic: _____

Main idea:

Detail 1:

Detail 2:

Detail 3:

◎⊙◎⊙◎⊙◎⊙◎⊙◎ Paragraph ⊙◎⊙◎⊙◎⊙◎⊙◎⊙◎⊙

Tips for Writing an Information Paragraph:
- Choose one topic to write about.
- Write a title for your paragraph.
- Write a topic sentence that tells your main idea.
- Write at least two detail sentences that tell facts about the main idea.
- Make sure your facts are correct.

DIRECTIONS

Choose a topic you would like to write about. Use your writing plan from page 112 as a guide for writing your information paragraph.

_____

_____

_____

_____

_____

_____

_____

_____

_____

_____

_____

Compare and Contrast Paragraph

In a **compare and contrast paragraph**, a writer can show how two people, places, or things are alike or different.

Example:

Geese and whales are different kinds of animals that migrate in large groups. Geese are birds, but whales are mammals. Birds spend much of their time in the air, but whales live in water. These animals are alike, though, because they both migrate thousands of miles. Both geese and whales travel in large groups to reach warmer weather. Geese migrate in groups called flocks. Whales travel in groups called pods.

How to Write a Compare and Contrast Paragraph
1. Write a topic sentence that names the subjects and tells briefly how they are alike and different.
2. Give examples in the detail sentences that clearly tell how the subjects are alike and different.
3. Write about the likenesses or the differences in the same order you named them in the topic sentence.

Compare and Contrast Paragraph, page 2

 **DIRECTIONS** Read the example compare and contrast paragraph on page 114. Then, answer the questions.

1. What two things are being compared?

_____

2. How are the two things different?

_____

_____

3. How are the two things alike?

_____

_____

DIRECTIONS Choose two things you want to write about. Write them on the lines below. Then, use the Venn diagram to help you plan your writing. List what is true only about A in the A circle. List what is true only about B in the B circle. List what is true about both A and B where the circles overlap.

A = _____

B = _____

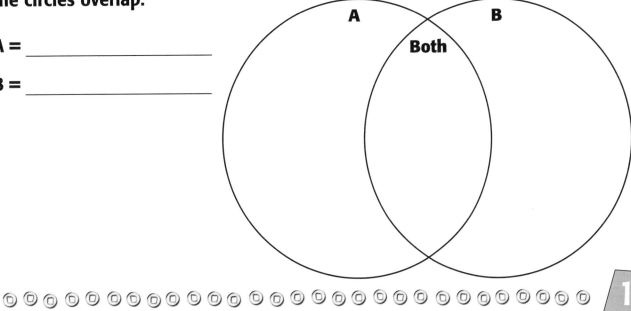

Tips for Writing a Compare and Contrast Paragraph:
• Think about your two subjects.
• Decide how the two subjects are alike and different.
• Write a topic sentence that tells how the two subjects are alike and different.
• Explain how the two subjects are alike.
• Explain how the two subjects are different.
• Write about the likenesses or the differences in the same order you named them in the topic sentence.

DIRECTIONS ➤ Choose two subjects you would like to compare and contrast. Use your Venn diagram from page 115 to write your compare and contrast paragraph.

_____

_____

_____

_____

_____

_____

_____

_____

_____

_____

Book Report

A **book report** tells about the important events in a book. It does not tell the ending. It also gives the writer's opinion of the book. Finally, it says whether others should read the book.
Example:

A Whale of a Story — title of report

The book <u>Humphrey the Lost Whale</u> by Wendy Tokuda and Richard Hall tells the true — title and author of book

story of a young whale that took a wrong turn. — main character

In the book, people were at first surprised and pleased to see a whale in San Francisco Bay. — setting

Then Humphrey headed up the Sacramento River. People soon realized he was lost. Hundreds of people worked together to get Humphrey back to the ocean. — main idea of book

This story will make you cheer. Read this book, and share it with a friend. — whether others should read it

How to Write a Book Report
1. Tell the title of the book. Underline it.
2. Give the author's name.
3. Tell about the book. Tell the main idea and interesting details. Do not tell the ending.
4. Give your opinion of the book.
5. Think of a title for your report.

Book Report, page 2

DIRECTIONS ➤ Read the example book report on page 117. Then, answer the questions.

1. What is the title of the book?

_____

2. Who wrote the book?

_____

3. Who is the main character of the book?

_____

4. Where does the book take place?

_____

5. Does the writer of the report think others should read the book? _____

DIRECTIONS ➤ Think of a book you would like to tell about. Then, use this writing plan to organize your report.

Title of book: _____

Author of book: _____

Main character of book: _____

Setting of book: _____

Main events of book: _____

_____

_____

_____

Should others read this book? _____

Book Report, page 3

Tips for Writing a Book Report:
- Choose one book to write about.
- Write a title for your report.
- Name the book and the author in your report.
- Name the main character and setting of the book.
- Tell the main events of the book, but do not tell the ending.
- Tell if you think others would like the book.

DIRECTIONS ➤ Choose a book you would like to write about. Use your writing plan from page 118 as a guide for writing your book report.

_____

_____

_____

_____

_____

_____

_____

_____

_____

_____

_____

Persuasive Paragraph

In a **persuasive paragraph**, a writer tries to make readers agree with his or her opinion.

Example:

Whale watching is good for people and for the environment. Many people have begun working for Earth-friendly causes after sailing near whales. Also, these intelligent animals seem to like the visitors. Tourists excitedly describe how whales come up to the boats to be touched. Most important, whale watching helps people learn how valuable and beautiful these mysterious mammals are. Everyone is helped by a whale-watching trip. Find out more about one today!

opinion in topic sentence

reasons and facts

strongest reason last

restated opinion or call for action

How to Write a Paragraph That Convinces

1. Write a topic sentence that tells your opinion or main idea.
2. Give reasons to support your main idea in the detail sentences. Save your strongest reason for last.
3. At the end of your paragraph, tell your feelings again. Ask your reader to feel the same way.

Persuasive Paragraph, page 2

DIRECTIONS > **Read the example persuasive paragraph on page 120. Then, answer the questions.**

1. What is the writer's main idea in this paragraph?

   _____

   _____

2. What are two reasons the writer gives to support the main idea?

   _____

   _____

3. What call for action does the writer use in the last sentence?

   _____

   _____

DIRECTIONS > **Think of something you feel strongly about. Then, use this writing plan to organize your persuasive paragraph.**

WRITING PLAN

Main idea: _____

Reason 1: _____

Reason 2: _____

Reason 3 (your strongest reason): _____

_____

_____

Call for action: _____

Tips for Writing a Persuasive Paragraph:
• Choose a topic that you feel strongly about.
• State your opinion in your topic sentence.
• Write good reasons to support your opinion.
• Try to have at least three good reasons.
• Save your strongest reason for last.
• At the end of your paragraph, restate your opinion. Tell the reader to take some action.

DIRECTIONS ➤ **Choose a topic that you have an opinion about. Use your writing plan from page 121 as a guide for writing your persuasive paragraph.**

_____

_____

_____

_____

_____

_____

_____

_____

_____

_____

_____

Writing for a Test

Some kinds of test questions ask you to write. These questions check to see if you can organize your thoughts and express your ideas. They also test to see if you can write for a specific purpose and use correct grammar. Here are some tips for writing better on a test.

Before the Test
- Listen carefully to all the directions your teacher or test giver gives you.
- Read all written directions carefully.
- Ask any questions you have. (You might not be allowed to talk once the test starts.)
- Have several pens or sharpened pencils on hand.
- If you are allowed, read each item on the test before you begin.

During the Test
- Take time to identify your task, audience, and purpose.
- Organize your thoughts before you write.
- Write neatly and clearly.
- If you need help, raise your hand. Don't call out or get up.

After the Test
- If you finish before time is up, go back and make final corrections.
- Follow the directions given at the beginning for what to do at the end of the test. You may have to sit quietly while others finish.

Timed Writing

You have probably taken timed tests before. What are some ways to do well during a timed writing test? Follow these tips to make a timed test go more smoothly:

- Stay calm. Take a deep breath and relax.
- For a writing test, remember to check your task and your purpose. (Unless you are told otherwise, your audience is the person who will read the test.)
- Plan how you will use your time. If this is a writing test, decide how much time you need to spend prewriting, drafting, revising, proofreading, and writing the final draft.
- If you begin to run out of time, decide if you can combine some steps. Your goal is to finish.

Written Prompts

A written prompt is a statement or a question that asks you to complete a writing task.

- A narrative prompt asks you to tell a story.
- A persuasive prompt asks you to convince the reader.
- An expository prompt asks you to inform or explain.
- A descriptive prompt asks you to describe something.

Picture Prompts

A picture prompt is a statement or question about a picture. It asks you to tell something about the picture. The prompt also tells the purpose for writing.

Using a Dictionary

The order of letters from *A* to *Z* is called **alphabetical order**. Words in a dictionary are listed in alphabetical order.

When words begin with the same letters, the next letter of the word is used to put the words in alphabetical order: <u>ca</u>pe, <u>ch</u>apel, <u>chi</u>me. Each word in the dictionary is an **entry word**.

There are two **guide words** at the top of every dictionary page. The word on the left is the first entry word on the page. The word on the right is the last entry word. All the other entry words on the page are in alphabetical order between the guide words.

 **DIRECTIONS** ➤ **Use this example dictionary page to answer the questions.**

cherry	chip
cher·ry [cher′ē] *n., pl.* **cher·ries** 1 A small, round, edible fruit, red, yellow, or nearly black in color, and having a single pit. 2 The tree bearing this fruit. 3 The wood of this tree. 4 A bright red color.	**child** [chīld] *n., pl.* **chil·dren** [chil′dren] 1 A baby. 2 A young boy or girl. 3 A son or daughter. 4 A person from a certain family.

1. What is the last entry word on this page? _____

How do you know? _____

2. What are the two guide words on this page? _____

_____

3. Which of these words would come before *cherry* in the dictionary:

carrot, corn, cactus, clover? _____

4. Would the word *chop* be on this page? _____

Using a Dictionary, page 2

A **syllable** is a word part that has only one vowel sound. Each entry word in the dictionary is divided into syllables.

A **pronunciation** follows each entry word. It shows how to say the word. It also shows the number of syllables in the word.

Examples:

phlox [fläks]   spinach [spin′ ich]

The **pronunciation key** lists the symbol for each sound. It also gives a familiar word in which the sound is heard. A pronunciation key usually appears on every other page of a dictionary.

a	add	i	it	o͞o	took	oi	oil
ā	ace	ī	ice	o͞o	pool	ou	pout
â	care	o	odd	u	up	ng	ring
ä	palm	ō	open	û	burn	th	thin
e	end	ô	order	yo͞o	fuse	th	this
ē	equal					zh	vision

ə = { a in above e in sicken i in possible
      o in melon u in circus }

 **DIRECTIONS** Read each pronunciation. Choose and circle the word that matches the pronunciation. Then, tell how many syllables are in each word.

1. klō′ vər   clever   cover   clover   _____

2. bēt   beet   bet   bait   _____

3. pik′ əl   pickle   pocket   pluck   _____

4. pâr   purr   pear   pour   _____

5. (h)wēt   what   wait   wheat   _____

Using a Dictionary, page 3

An **entry** is all the information about an entry word.

A **definition** is the meaning of a word. Many words have more than one definition. Each definition is numbered.

A definition is often followed by an **example** that shows how to use the word.

spin [spin] *v.* **1** To draw out and twist (as cotton or flax) into thread. **2** To make fibers into threads or yarn by spinning. **3** To make something, as a web or cocoon, from sticky fibers from an insect's body: Wolf spiders do not spin webs. **4** To turn or whirl about; rotate: to spin a top. **5** To make up a story or tale.

DIRECTIONS Use the entry for *spin* to answer the questions.

1. How many definitions are given for the entry word? _____

2. For which definition is there an example sentence? _____

3. How many syllables does the entry word have? _____

4. What information is given in brackets [ ]? _____

5. Which definition of *spin* is used in this sentence?

Rumpelstiltskin could spin straw into gold. _____

Using a Thesaurus

A **thesaurus** is a book that tells synonyms, words that have nearly the same meaning, and antonyms, words that mean the opposite of a word. Many thesauruses are like dictionaries. The entry words are listed in dark print in alphabetical order. Guide words at the top of the page tell which words can be found on the page. Good writers use a thesaurus to find interesting words.

give   **goal**

glad *syn* cheerful, happy, jolly, joyful, lighthearted, merry, pleased
ant blue, downcast, glum, sad, unhappy

 ➤ **Use a thesaurus. Replace the underlined word with a synonym or antonym. Write the new word on the line.**

1. Dan will <u>get</u> a baby duck in the spring.

synonym _____

2. Dan is very <u>lucky</u>.

synonym _____

3. A baby deer would make a <u>bad</u> pet.

synonym _____

4. Baby raccoons are the <u>most</u> popular pets.

antonym _____

5. It is very <u>kind</u> to keep raccoons in a cage.

antonym _____

Using an Encyclopedia

An **encyclopedia** is a set of books that has facts on many subjects. Each book in a set is called a volume. The volumes list subjects in alphabetical order.

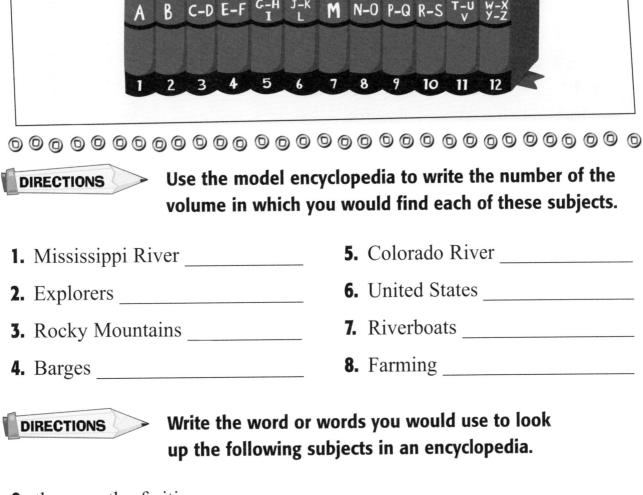

DIRECTIONS → Use the model encyclopedia to write the number of the volume in which you would find each of these subjects.

1. Mississippi River _____

2. Explorers _____

3. Rocky Mountains _____

4. Barges _____

5. Colorado River _____

6. United States _____

7. Riverboats _____

8. Farming _____

DIRECTIONS → Write the word or words you would use to look up the following subjects in an encyclopedia.

9. the growth of cities _____

10. the logging business _____

11. mountains in the United States _____

12. American ships _____

13. rivers of America _____

14. the uses of water _____

Using the Internet

The computer can help you to do research. You can use the Internet to find almost any information. The key to finding information is to know which keywords to type. Here are some hints to speed up the search.

How to Use the Internet
1. Make a list of keywords or names.
2. Type in two or three keywords.
3. Type in different combinations of keywords until the topic titles focus on the information you need.

 **Write the keywords you would use to search for these subjects.**

1. author Shel Silverstein _____

2. time a movie starts at the theater _____

3. the weather _____

4. download a new computer game _____

5. how to add fractions _____

6. where to buy shoes _____

7. which Native American groups lived in your area _____

8. how to get to a place _____

9. what to see in a city you would like to visit _____

10. what kind of dog you might like _____

Parts of a Book

The **title page** tells the name of a book. It gives the name of the author. It also tells the name of the company that published the book. The **table of contents** comes after the title page. It lists the titles of the chapters or units in the book. It also lists the page on which each new part begins. Everything in the book is listed in the order in which it appears.

An **index** is a list of all the topics in a book. It is in alphabetical order. It lists the page or pages on which each topic appears.

 **DIRECTIONS** **Use the example book pages to answer the questions.**

ART PROJECTS AT THE BEACH by Sandy Shore Crafts Books, Inc.	**Contents** Getting Started . . . 8 Shell Art . . . . 10 Sand Art . . . . 32 Sea-Plant and Rock Crafts 50	Beaches, 8–10, 26, 29 Plants, 50–54, 60–62 Rocks, 50–54, 59–62 Sand, 8–12, 32–49 Shells, 8, 10–30
title page	**table of contents**	**index**

1. What is the title of the book? _____

2. Who wrote the book? _____

3. What company published this book? _____

4. What is the first chapter in the book? _____

5. What chapter begins on page 32? _____

6. On what pages would you find facts about beaches? _____

Kinds of Books

Fiction books tell stories. They tell about make-believe people and things.
Example:
   Charlotte's Web, a book about a talking spider

Nonfiction books tell facts about real people, things, or events. A nonfiction book that tells about the life of a real person is called a biography.
Example:
   Spider Silk, facts about how spiders spin webs

Reference books are often in a special section in the library. In this section you will find the dictionary, thesaurus, encyclopedia, almanac, atlas, and other books. All these books contain factual information. They are nonfiction books.

DIRECTIONS ▷ **Tell if each book below is *fiction* or *nonfiction*.**

1. a book of maps _____

2. a true book about a famous scientist's life _____

3. a book of facts about insects of the world _____

4. a story about Lydia, a hamster that talks _____

5. a book of word meanings _____

6. a book of poems about dragons _____

7. a book about students at a school for wizards _____

8. a book of folk tales _____

Reading for Information

Skimming is a quick way to read. When you skim a paragraph, you look for its main idea. The main idea is the most important idea in the paragraph.

Scanning is also a quick reading method. When you scan a page, you look it over to find a particular fact.

 **DIRECTIONS** Skim this paragraph. Then, circle the sentence below that best states the main idea.

The months of January and March were named after Roman gods long ago. The month of January was named for Janus, the god of beginnings. March was named for Mars, the god of war.

1. Some months are named after Roman gods.

2. The names of the months come from unusual words.

3. The Romans named the months long ago.

 **DIRECTIONS** Scan this paragraph. Then, answer the questions.

Other months' names came from Latin words used by Romans. April comes from the Latin word *aperio*, which means "to open." The last four months of the year come from Latin words for numbers: *septem* (seven), *octo* (eight), *novem* (nine), *decem* (ten).

4. What does the Latin word *aperio* mean?

_____

5. What Latin word means the number nine?

_____

Fact or Opinion

Which of these sentences is a fact? Which is an opinion?

1. There are many different kinds of dogs.
2. I think dogs are the best kind of pets.

If you decided that sentence 1 is a fact, you are right. A **fact** is a statement that can be proved.

Sentence 2 is a nonfact, or an opinion. An **opinion** is what someone thinks, feels, or believes. Words like *think*, *believe*, and *feel* are words often used with opinions. These are clues that what the author is saying is an opinion.

Writers often try to get you to agree with their opinions. It is important for you to know the difference between a fact and an opinion.

DIRECTIONS ▷ **Read each statement and decide if it is a fact or an opinion. Write *fact* or *opinion* on the line.**

1. I feel that basketball is the best sport. _____

2. A zoo is a place to see many animals. _____

3. There are three feet in one yard. _____

4. I think math is the hardest subject. _____

5. A day is shorter than a week. _____

DIRECTIONS ▷ **Follow the directions to write complete sentences.**

6. Write a fact about your home. _____

_____

7. Write an opinion about your home. _____

_____

Taking Notes

A writer takes good **notes** to remember the facts he or she finds when doing research for a report.
Example:

Wild Travelers, by George Laycock, page 67
Where do male fur seals migrate to?
    to Gulf of Alaska
    travel 400–500 miles from winter home

How to Take Notes

1. Write a question. Then, find a book to answer the question.
2. List the title of the book, the author, and the pages where you find facts.
3. Write answers to your question. Write only the facts you need for your report.
4. Write the information in your own words. Write sentences or short groups of words.

 **DIRECTIONS**   **Read the paragraph. Take notes on the facts you would use in a report about female fur seals.**

Female fur seals do an amazing thing. Each year in the fall, they migrate 3,000 miles. They leave the Pribilof Islands and swim all the way to southern California.

_____

_____

_____

_____

Summary

A **summary** is a short sentence or paragraph that tells the main facts or ideas in a story or selection. To summarize any writing, you must pay attention to the details. Using the question words *who, what, where, when,* and *why* can help you find the important details to include in a summary. A summary table can help you organize the information to write a summary.

DIRECTIONS Read the paragraph. Then, complete the summary table.

People who plan to camp should be prepared for some crawly company. Spiders surprise campers by appearing in unusual places. Spiders might be found on early morning canoe trips. They might jump out of boots, drop from trees, or crawl out from under rocks. Spiders crawl into these different spaces looking for a safe place to spin a web to catch food to eat.

Who:	Summary:
What:	
Where:	
When:	
Why:	

Outline

A writer uses an **outline** to put the notes for a research report in order.
Example:

    Migrating Seals
    I. Live in Alaska
    II. Travel south in fall

How to Write an Outline
1. Write a title telling the subject of your report.
2. Write the main topics. Use a Roman numeral and a period before each topic.
3. Begin each main topic with a capital letter.

 **Write these main topics in correct outline form.**
Use the title below for your outline.

Migrating Monarch Butterflies
migrate south from Canada and northern United States
spend winter in southern United States and Mexico
return home in spring

_____

_____

_____

_____

_____

_____

Rough Draft

A writer quickly puts all of his or her ideas on paper in a **rough draft**.

How to Write a Rough Draft
1. Read your outline and notes. Keep them near you as you write.
2. Follow your outline to write a rough draft. Do not add anything that is not on your outline. Do not leave out anything.
3. Write one paragraph for each Roman numeral in your outline.
4. Write freely. Do not worry about mistakes now. You will make changes later.

 **Choose one of the outlines below. Write a topic sentence for each paragraph of a rough draft.**

1. Migrating Swallows
   I. Fly long distances to get away from cold
   II. Migrate by day
   III. Travel 10,000 miles

2. Migrating Geese
   I. Live in the United States and Canada
   II. Fly in groups
   III. Fly as far south as Mexico

_____

_____

_____

_____

Research Report

First, a writer makes all the changes in the rough draft.
Then, he or she writes the final copy of the **research report**.
Example:

Migrating Seals

Seals are migrating animals. Fur seals from the Pribilof Islands near Alaska migrate every fall.

Female and male fur seals migrate to different places. In the fall, female fur seals swim 3,000 miles to southern California. The male fur seals migrate to the Gulf of Alaska. They travel only 400 to 500 miles from their summer homes.

How to Write a Research Report
1. Write the title of your report.
2. Write the report. Use your rough draft.
3. Make all the changes you marked on your rough draft.
4. Indent the first sentence of each paragraph.

DIRECTIONS ▷ **On the lines below write some ideas of subjects you would like to research. Take notes on one of the subjects. Write an outline and a rough draft. Then, write a report.**

_____

_____

_____

Analyzing a Research Report

A research report gives facts about one topic.
It usually has more than one paragraph.
It has a title that tells about the topic.

◎◎◎◎◎◎◎◎◎◎◎◎◎◎◎◎◎◎◎◎◎◎◎◎◎◎◎◎◎◎

DIRECTIONS ▷ **Read this research report. Answer the questions.**

Colds

A cold is caused by a virus. No one really knows how to prevent colds. Getting wet or chilled does not directly give you a cold. A chill, however, might put you in a weaker state than usual. Then, if a cold is going around, you will be more likely to get it.

Colds are usually caught by being near someone who already has one. The easiest way to catch a cold is from someone's sneeze. One person with a cold in a crowd can give it to many other people just by sneezing. If you have a cold, you should stay away from other people.

1. What is the topic of this report? _____

2. Write the sentence that states the main idea.

_____

_____

3. What is one detail about the main idea?

_____

_____

4. What might the topic of another paragraph in this research paper be?

_____

◎◎◎◎◎◎◎◎◎◎◎◎◎◎◎◎◎◎◎◎◎◎◎◎◎◎◎◎

Answer Key

Unit 1

Page 6
1. flute, 2. musician, 3. stage, 4. tree, 5. girl, 6. forest, 7.–9. Sentences will vary.

Page 7
Common nouns: problem, school, miles, pool, dog, school, pool, brother, car, evening, practice
Proper nouns: Maren, Kona Kai Swim Team, Collins School, Miller Avenue, Kona Express Bus, Leif, Burger Pit Restaurant
Sentences will vary.

Page 8
1. common: clockmaker; proper: Levi Hutchins, 2. common: person; proper: Concord, New Hampshire, 3. proper: Hutchins, 4. common: fellow, sun, 5. common: people, sky, 6. common: man, idea, clock, 7. common: machine, bell, 8. common: owner, piece, time, 9. common: chime, 10. common: invention; proper: Hutchins

Page 9
Proper Nouns
Person: Serena, Riane, Mr. Williams; Place: Vallco Concert Hall; Thing: Shadygrove Band
Common Nouns
Person: musicians, leader; Place: school, home; Thing: day, talent, group

Page 10
1. plural: badgers, diggers, 2. singular: badger, hole, 3. singular: mammal; plural: claws, 4. singular: animal, enemy, 5. singular: mole; plural: paws, 6. plural: legs, shovels, 7. plural: tunnels, bushes, trees, 8. singular: creature, 9. singular: digger, world, 10. plural: badgers, moles, diggers

Page 11
1. animals, 2. farmers, 3. chickens, 4. ducks, 5. swans, 6. cows, 7. horses, 8. lambs, 9. goats, 10. pigs, 11. piglets

Page 12
1. glasses, 2. dishes, 3. foxes, 4. patches, 5. matches, 6. dresses, 7. lunches, 8. taxes, 9. classes, 10. bushes, 11.–15. Sentences will vary.

Page 13
1. cities, 2. families, 3. parties, 4. butterflies, 5. flies, 6. puppies, 7. bunnies, 8. babies, 9. daisies, 10. stories

Page 14
1. child, 2. man, 3. woman, 4. goose, 5. mice, 6. ox, 7. mouse, 8. geese, 9. children, 10. teeth

Page 15
Sentences may vary. 1. Hope's kite is bright yellow., 2. The kite's tail is much too long., 3. It will get stuck in that tree's branches., 4. The girl's parents have kites, too., 5. Her mother's kite looks like a dragon., 6. Her dad's kite is shaped like a box., 7. Hope wants to fly her friend's kite., 8. The park's fields made flying kites fun.

Page 16
Paragraph: chickens', animals', foxes'
1. squirrels', 2. brothers', 3. dogs', 4. trees'

Page 17
1. table's; singular, 2. dog's; singular, 3. families'; plural, 4. picnickers'; plural, 5. blackberries'; plural, 6. Adam's; singular, 7. grandparents'; plural, 8. bike's; singular

Page 18
1. He; Little Elk, 2. She; Little Elk's mother, 3. He; Little Elk, 4. It; paint

Page 19
1. He, 2. her, 3. him, 4. She, 5. It, 6. he

Page 20
1. We, 2. them, 3. They, 4. them, 5. They, 6. us

Page 21
1. They, 2. they, 3. It, 4. She, 5. They

Page 22
Paragraph: singular: I, She, I, You, He; plural: They
Chart: I, Meredyth; She, mother; They, pictures; I, Meredyth; You, Meredyth; He, Dad

Page 23
us, them, her, him, it, them, him, They, them

Page 24
1. My friends and I, 2. us, 3. Nell and I, 4. Casey and I, 5. me, 6. me, 7. I, 8. me, 9. Mom and me, 10. My parents and I

Page 25
1. her, 2. our, 3. My, 4. your, 5. his, 6. their, 7. my, 8. its, 9. your, 10. My, 11. her

Page 26
1. It's, 2. You're, 3. they're, 4. they've, 5. it's, 6. I'll, 7. you're, 8. You'll

Page 27
1. small, 2. Many, 3. main, 4. heavy, 5. split, 6. double, 7. central, 8. other, 9. wooden, 10. big

Page 28
1. Two, 2. Several, 3. Some, 4. few, 5. eight, 6.–8. Sentences will vary.

Page 29
1. tiny; computers, 2. secret; pouch, 3. careful; notes, 4. difficult; mysteries, 5. lost; diamonds, 6. famous; parrot, 7. important; key, 8. embarrassed; friend, 9.–10. Sentences will vary.

Page 30
1. beautiful; Yosemite Park, 2. incredible; views, 3. difficult; mountain, 4. taller; tree, 5. blue; sky, 6. tiny; houses, 7. sick; man, 8. mean; dog, 9. sweet; flower, 10. soft; cat

Page 31
Paragraph: an, the, the, a, the, a, an, a, the
1. a, 2. a, 3. an, 4. an, 5. A

Page 32
1. richer, 2. poorest, 3. younger, 4. fancier, 5. hungrier, 6. grandest

Page 33
1. most, 2. more, 3. most, 4. more, 5. most, 6. most, 7. more, 8. most, 9. more, 10. most

Page 34
Paragraph: more interesting, rarer, most difficult, bolder, easier
1. friendlier, 2. happier, 3. more, 4. easier, 5. noisiest

Page 35
1. begin, 2. changes, 3. grows, 4. kick, 5. develop, 6. breathe, 7. loses, 8. becomes, 9. climbs, 10. appears

Page 36
1. peek, 2. covers, 3. go, 4. close, 5. walk, 6. crunch, 7. nips, 8. build, 9. return, 10. remove

Page 37
1. floated, 2. landed, 3. disappeared,
4. passed, 5. taped, 6. played,
7. noticed, 8. changed, 9. soared,
10. waited

Page 38
1. has; owned, 2. have; traveled,
3. had; soared, 4. have; wanted,
5. had; looked, 6. has; landed, 7.
have; replaced, 8. had; painted, 9.
have; called, 10. has; planned

Page 39
Paragraph
Main verbs: traveled, visited, read,
planned, given, stayed, written
Helping verbs: has, have, have, had,
has, have, has
1. has, 2. has, 3. have, 4. have
Sentences will vary.

Page 40
1. drive, 2. drives, 3. drink, 4. drinks,
5. play, 6. chase, 7. watches, 8. takes,
9. plays, 10. watch

Page 41
1. rained; ed, 2. closed; d, 3. crashed;
ed, 4. barked; ed, 5. watched; ed,
6. poured; ed, 7. leaked; ed, 8. placed;
d, 9. started; ed, 10. listened; ed

Page 42
1. eat, 2. live, 3. spends, 4. covers,
5. swims, 6. visited, 7. helped,
8. enjoyed, 9. cooked, 10. liked

Page 43
1. driven, 2. came, 3. ate, 4. went,
5. drove, 6. came, 7. did, 8. go

Page 44
1. gave, 2. wrote, 3. knew, 4. taken,
5. grew, 6. took, 7. ate, 8. took,
9. eaten, 10. written

Page 45
1. live; action, 2. is; be, 3. are; be,
4. use; action, 5. are; be, 6. were; be,
7. is; be, 8. am; be, 9. are; be,
10. build; action

Page 46
1. everywhere; where, 2. here; where,
3. often; when, 4. never; when,
5. always; when, 6. often,
7. sometimes, 8. Soon

Page 47
1. swiftly, 2. quickly, 3. Breathlessly,
4. Luckily, 5. excitedly, 6. foolishly,
7. exactly, 8. Fortunately, 9. barely,
10. happily

Page 48
Paragraph: downstairs, often,
carefully, cleverly
1.–5. Sentences will vary.

Page 49
1. correct, 2. well, 3. well, 4. good,
5. correct, 6. good, 7. well, 8. good

Unit 2

Page 50
Students should underline: 1, 3, 5, 7.
9.–10. Sentences will vary.

Page 51
1. subject, 2. subject, 3. predicate,
4. subject, 5. predicate, 6. predicate,
7. subject, 8. predicate, 9. subject,
10. predicate

Page 52
1. Some seeds, 2. Dandelion seeds,
3. The wind, 4. They, 5. Pioneers,
6. These settlers, 7. Some families,
8. The wilderness

Page 53
1. climbed Mount Whitney, 2. is in
California, 3. went there with her
father, 4. climbed for one whole day,
5. took pictures of snow at the top,
6. went rafting on the Snake River,
7. bucked like a wild horse, 8. loved
the exciting ride

Page 54
1. subject: New York City; predicate:
is the largest city in the United States.
2. subject: More than 7 million
people; predicate: live in New York
City. 3. subject: New Yorkers;
predicate: come from many different
backgrounds. 4. subject: The subway
system; predicate: runs on about 230
miles of track. 5. subject: The city;
predicate: is a center for trade,
business, and the arts. 6. subject:
Millions of people; predicate: visit
New York City every year. 7. subject:
Theater; predicate: is one of the city's
most popular art forms. 8. subject:
Many visitors; predicate: attend
Broadway shows. 9. subject: One tall
building in New York City; predicate:
is the Empire State Building.
10. subject: The Statue of Liberty;
predicate: stands on an island in New
York Harbor. 11. subject: This
monument; predicate: is a symbol of
freedom. 12. subject: Tourists;
predicate: take pictures of the statue.

Page 55
1. Do you like gardens?; Q, 2. We
planted vegetables here.; S, 3. Do the
plants need water?; Q, 4. Who will
pull the weeds?; Q, 5. These tomatoes
look good.; S, 6. Are they ripe?; Q,
7. This tomato is bright red.; S

Page 56
1. Watch my pet fish.; C, 2. He's
amazing!; E, 3. See how he follows
my directions.; C, 4. Swim through
the hoop, Finny.; C, 5. Now dive to
the bottom.; C, 6. You're terrific,
Finny!; E, 7. Swim around in big
circles., C

Page 57
1. ? , 2. . , 3. . , 4. ? , 5. . or ! ,
6. Most early people used combs.
The only ones who didn't were the
Britons., 7. Does it make you wonder
how they looked? The Britons left
their hair messy., 8. I comb my hair
every day. Do you?

Page 58
1. am, 2. are, 3. is, 4. is, 5. are, 6. is,
7. am, 8. were, 9. was, 10. was,
11. were, 12. were

Page 59
1. Kathy was tired and wanted her
lunch., 2. She turned smoothly in the
water and headed for the other end of
the pool., 3. Kathy wanted to win and
hoped to set records., 4. Kathy won
many races and got many awards.

Page 60
1. Guppies and goldfish are pets for
fish tanks., 2. Catfish and snails clean
harmful moss from the tank., 3. Black
mollies and goldfish are lovely fish.,
4. Guppies and black mollies have
live babies., 5. Zebra fish and
angelfish lay eggs.

Page 61
1. Inventions make our lives easier,
and we take them for granted., 2. We
get cold, and we turn on a heater.,
3. Long ago people got cold, and they
sat around a fire., 4. A very long time
ago, people had no fire, and they
stayed cold., 5. Our heater works,
and we stay warm.

Page 62
1. Pet mice can be black, red, or
silver., 2. Other colors for mice
include gray, cream, and white., 3. A
mouse can chew on wood, nuts, and
twigs., 4. Mice clean their own
bodies, faces, and ears., 5. Soup cans
are good resting places for pet mice,
hamsters, and gerbils.

Page 63

Sentences will vary. Possible responses are given.
1. The tiny hummingbird built a dainty nest., **2.** She found a large tree in a quiet place., **3.** She wanted her nest to be far away from curious cats., **4.** She laid three eggs and sat on them patiently., **5.** Soon the eggs hatched, and the babies cried hungrily for food.

Page 64

1. The baby opened the cabinet. She took out all the pots., **2.** The mother came into the kitchen. She saw the mess., **3.** The mother smiled at the baby. She asked if it was fun., **4.** The baby smiled back. She was having a good time., **5.** The mother sat on the floor. She played with the baby.

Unit 3

Page 65

1. Our dentist is Dr. Ellen J. Oldham., **2.** She works with Dr. Karl V. Swift., **3.** Dad's friend Chan works in the office., **4.** Sometimes Miss Kitazawa works there, too., **5.** My sister Leah had her checkup yesterday., **6.** Today Mrs. Kim and Ms. Ozario will see Dr. Oldham., **7.** Mr. Kramer sees Dr. Oldham every three months., **8.** Max and I went to visit Mrs. Delgado.

Page 66

1. Zion National Park, **2.** State Street, **3.** South America, **4.** Mississippi River, **5.** Handy Hardware Store, **6.–10.** Sentences will vary. Be sure each sentence has a proper noun.

Page 67

1. February, **2.** Monday, **3.** Labor Day, **4.** November, **5.** Saturday, **6.** Thanksgiving Day, **7.–12.** Sentences will vary. Be sure each answer is the name of a day, month, or holiday.

Page 68

1. Pompeii, **2.** August, **3.** Italy, **4.** Mount Vesuvius, **5.** Mediterranean Sea, **6.** Naples, **7.** Metropolitan Museum, **8.** Europe

Page 69

1. Manny and Tony go to the beach every day., **2.** Do not step on the crabs., **3.** Dr. Quick looked at Mr. Smith's toe., **4.** Mrs. Smith found a bandage., **5.** Dr. Quick helped Mr. Smith.
Beach Activities
 I. Play in the waves
 II. Look for shells
 III. Have a picnic

Page 70

1. Circle Rd., **2.** July, **3.** Dr. Homer A. Mancebo or Dr. H. A. Mancebo, **4.** Tues., **5.** 493 Dinosaur Ave., **6.** Mr. W. Ambrose, **7.** Sat., Apr. 13, **8.** Angela P. Mills or A. P. Mills, **9.** Mon., **10.** Miss Cynthia A. Forbes, **11.** Feb. 28, **12.** Deerpath Rd.

Page 71

Sentences will vary. Be sure each answer begins with Yes, No, or Well.

Page 72

1. An octopus has eight legs, large eyes, and strong jaws., **2.** An octopus eats clams, crabs, and lobsters., **3.** Octopuses live along the coasts of Hawaii, Australia, and China., **4.** The desert seems to shimmer, shine, and bubble in the hot sun., **5.** Sometimes the wind will blow, swirl, or whip the sand around.

Page 73

Commas needed after New Delhi, May 3, Chandra, and Sincerely

Page 74

1. Meghan and her family took the 8:30 PM train., **2.** At 7:15 the next morning, they ate breakfast., **3.** The train pulled into Union Station at 8:45 AM., **4.** Meghan didn't want to waste time., **5.** She wasn't interested in looking at the city from their windows., **6.** Meghan's cousins met them at the hotel., **7.** Her cousins' rooms overlooked the lake., **8.** Meghan's father took them to the fair., **9.** They stayed at the fair until 9:00 PM., **10.** Meghan couldn't stay awake on the ride home.

Page 75

1. shouldn't, **2.** isn't, **3.** aren't, **4.** don't, **5.** can't, **6.** hadn't, **7.** won't, **8.** wasn't, **9.** don't, **10.** hasn't

Page 76

1. Lily said, "Let's go to the beach.", **2.** Jeff exclaimed, "That's a great idea!", **3.** correct, **4.** Uncle Bill said, "Well, I'd love to go to the beach.", **5.** Jeff asked, "Where is our big beach ball?", **6.** correct, **7.** Dad reminded them, "Don't forget your towels.", **8.** Lily shouted, "This is great!"

Page 77

1. Chet got a book called The Story of Baseball from the library today., **2.** The first story, titled "In the Beginning," starts in 1846., **3.** The last story is called "Why Is Baseball So Popular?", **4.** Last week Chet read a book called Pioneers of Baseball by Robert Smith., **5.** His favorite story, "The One and Only," is about Babe Ruth.

Unit 4

Page 78

1. outdoor; out, door; out of a house, outside, **2.** playground; play, ground; a place to play, **3.** overcoat; over, coat; a coat worn over a sweater or jacket, **4.** lightweight; light, weight; not heavy, **5.** mealtime; meal, time; a time to eat a meal, **6.** afternoon; after, noon; after 12:00 PM, **7.** mockingbird; mocking, bird; a bird that sounds like other birds, **8.** treetop; tree, top; the top of a tree

Page 79

Check that the correct synonym is used in the rewritten sentences.
1. nearly, **2.** large, **3.** know, **4.** whole

Page 80

1. hardest; easiest, **2.** toward; away, **3.** clean; dirty, **4.** remember; forget, **5.** good; bad, **6.** fresh; old, **7.** small; large

Page 81

1. unusual, **2.** impatient, **3.** disliked, **4.** unlucky, **5.** impossible

Page 82

1. inventor, **2.** useful, **3.** helper, **4.** fearless, **5.** joyful, **6.** successful

Page 83

1. a, **2.** b, **3.** b, **4.** a, **5.** a, **6.** b, **7.** Sentences will vary.

Page 84

1. days, **2.** pears, **3.** flour, **4.** seem, **5.** dough, **6.** eight, **7.** I, **8.** right, **9.** piece, **10.** fair, **11.** One; won, **12.** past; passed, **13.** find; fined

Page 85

1. to, **2.** too, **3.** to, **4.** to, **5.** two, **6.** too, **7.** two, **8.** to, **9.** two, **10.** too

Page 86

1. It's, **2.** It's, **3.** It's, **4.** its, **5.** its, **6.** Its, **7.** It's, **8.** It's, **9.** its, **10.** It's

Page 87

1. You're, **2.** your, **3.** you're, **4.** your, **5.** you're, **6.** Your, **7.** You're, **8.** your, **9.** you're, **10.** you're

Page 88

1. their, **2.** They're, **3.** They're, **4.** there, **5.** their, **6.** there, **7.** their, **8.** there, **9.** They're, **10.** their

Page 89

1. look, **2.** feel, **3.** sound, **4.** look, **5.** sound, **6.** look, **7.** look, **8.** taste, **9.** feel, **10.** smell

Page 90
1. fog, cat: Both are quiet, and you can't hear them coming., 2. fog, blanket: Both cover something so you can't see what's underneath., 3. tree, umbrella: Both provide shelter., 4. moon, Grandma: Both make the speaker feel good by seeming to smile., 5. lake, mirror: Both the lake and the mirror reflect light., 6. grasshoppers, echo: Both seem to respond right away., 7. knife, boat: Both move quietly and easily.

Page 91
1. strolls, 2. watches, 3. enjoys, 4. pass, 5. sees, 6. touch, 7. takes, 8. fill, 9. teaches, 10. understands

Page 92
Answers will vary. Possible responses are given.
1. plays, 2. waters, 3. grow, 4. hears, 5. swim, 6. hops, 7. counts, 8. walks

Unit 5

Page 93
Some hunters use their teeth to catch food., Other hunters run to trap food., Some jump on insects to catch them.

Page 94
Answers may vary.
1. The second paragraph is more interesting because there are more details and examples., 2. Though they can also see well in the daytime, owls are known for seeing at night., 3. Responses will vary, but should correctly give a detail from the paragraph., 4. If you stood in the sunlight and your friend stood in the shade, an owl could see each of you well.

Page 95
Answers may vary.
   A sighted person can imagine what it is like to be blind. Put a scarf over your eyes to block out light. Try to figure out what different foods are. Pretend to pay for something with coins. Try to walk into another room and sit at a table. Blind people can do all these things and more.

Page 97
1. to tell how he got his name, 2. The writer tells a story about himself., 3. At first, he does not know how he got his name.

Page 100
1. Answers will vary., 2. head, said; that, cat, 3. an alarm. **Poem:** Answers will vary.

Page 103
1. fall, 2. Answers will vary: crisp, cool, thump, big, tall, little, sweet-smelling jelly, high-stepping, squealed, 3. Answers will vary.

Page 106
1. Mimi, 2. 27 Green Street, Burlington, NC 27215, 3. Dear Grandma, 4. her hamster

Page 109
1. how to make a volcano, 2. a pan, a plastic bottle, red food coloring, a bottle of vinegar, baking soda, and some sand, 3. First, add a few drops of food coloring to the vinegar., 4. First, Next, Finally

Page 112
1. Mount Cameroon is a special mountain in Africa., 2. more than 30 years ago, 3. Answers will vary.

Page 115
1. geese and whales, 2. They are different kinds of animals, and they live in different places., 3. They both migrate long distances in large groups.

Page 118
1. Humphrey the Lost Whale, 2. Wendy Tokuda and Richard Hall, 3. Humphrey, a young whale, 4. San Francisco Bay, 5. yes

Page 121
1. Whale watching is good for people and for the environment., 2. Answers may vary: People work for Earth-friendly causes after watching whales.; People learn how special whales are., 3. Find out more about a whale-watching trip today.

Unit 6

Page 125
1. chip; because it is the second guide word, 2. cherry, chip, 3. carrot, cactus, 4. no

Page 126
1. clover; 2, 2. beet; 1, 3. pickle; 2, 4. pear; 1, 5. wheat; 1

Page 127
1. 5, 2. 3, 3. 1, 4. pronunciation, 5. 2

Page 128
Answers will vary. 1. purchase, 2. fortunate, 3. awful, 4. least, 5. unkind

Page 129
1. 7, 2. 4, 3. 10, 4. 2, 5. 3, 6. 11, 7. 10, 8. 4, 9. cities, 10. logging, 11. mountains, United States, 12. ships, America 13. rivers, America 14. water

Page 130
1. Silverstein, 2. movies, 3. weather, 4. computers; games, 5. math; fractions, 6. shoes, 7. Native Americans, 8. maps, 9. the name of the city, 10. dogs

Page 131
1. Art Projects at the Beach, 2. Sandy Shore, 3. Crafts Books, Inc., 4. Getting Started, 5. Sand Art, 6. 8–10, 26, 29

Page 132
1. nonfiction, 2. nonfiction, 3. nonfiction, 4. fiction, 5. nonfiction, 6. fiction, 7. fiction, 8. fiction

Page 133
Students should circle sentence 1., 4. to open, 5. *novem*

Page 134
1. opinion, 2. fact, 3. fact, 4. opinion, 5. fact, 6.–7. Sentences will vary.

Page 135
Notes should include: each fall, migrate 3,000 miles, Pribilof Islands to southern California

Page 136
Answers may vary. Who: Campers; What: Spiders; Where: In unusual places, such as in canoes and boots; When: At different times; Why: Looking for a safe place to spin a web to catch food; Summary: Spiders spin webs in unusual places to catch food. Campers may be surprised by spiders at any time.

Page 137
Migrating Monarch Butterflies
   I. Migrate south from Canada and northern United States
   II. Spend winter in southern United States and Mexico
III. Return home in spring

Page 138
Topic sentences will vary, but should be complete sentences. Examples for Migrating Swallows: 1. Migrating swallows fly long distances to get away from the cold., 2. Migrating swallows migrate by day., 3. Migrating swallows travel 10,000 miles.; Examples for Migrating Geese: 1. Migrating geese live in the United States and Canada., 2. Migrating geese fly in groups., 3. Migrating geese fly as far south as Mexico.

Page 140
1. colds, 2. A cold is caused by a virus., 3. Answers will vary., 4. Answers will vary.